Major Taylor in Australia

Jim Fitzpatrick

Star Hill Studio

To Roey

Published in Australia in 2011
by Star Hill Studio Pty Ltd
ABN 12 135 353 249
342 Mt. Kilcoy Road,
Kilcoy, Queensland, 4515, Australia
www.starhillstudio.com.au

Copyright © Star Hill Studio Pty Ltd 2011

ISBN: 978-0-9807480-2-4

National Library of Australia Cataloguing-in-publication entry
    Author: Fitzpatrick, Jim, 1943-
    Title: Major Taylor in Australia/Jim Fitzpatrick.
    ISBN: 9780980748024 (pbk.)
    Notes: Includes bibliographical references and index.
    Subjects: Taylor, Major, 1878-1932.
               African American cyclists--Australia.
               Bicycle racing--Australia--History.
               Cyclists--United States.
               Cyclists--Australia.
               Discrimination in sports--Australia.
    Dewey Number: 796.62092

Designed by Roey Fitzpatrick

Contents

An Extraordinary Athlete

For one and a half decades, from 1896, spectators filled stadium after stadium in North America, Europe, the United Kingdom and Australasia to watch Major Taylor, a black American cyclist, race. He was the highest paid and most famous athlete in what was then the world's most popular and lucrative sport. To give perspective, Honus Wagner's 1908 salary of $10,000 to play baseball in America (soon matched by Ty Cobb) was considered sensational, a landmark in American professional sports history. In 1903 Major Taylor's earnings approached $50,000.

The Major's earnings stand the test of time. In November, 2009 Tiger Woods' combined appearance fee and first prize at the Australian Masters Golf Tournament was AU$3,250,000, 51 times an average Australian's earnings. In 1903 Major Taylor left Australia with £4,000 in appearance fees and winnings, 22 times the average Australian's wage that year. That is the November 2009 equivalent of AU$1,400,000.

With respect to fame, however, time has taken its toll.

Hovering over Major Taylor was the intense racial prejudice of that era, particularly in the United States. The difficulties associated with travelling and competing, combined with the bigotry, hatred, threats and unfairness of his competitors, eventually became intolerable. It ultimately forced Taylor off American cycle tracks and out of the country.

It was in Australia that it came to a head. Hugh McIntosh, an Australian promoter, invited Taylor Down Under for the 1903 summer racing season. He created the world's richest bicycle race as an inducement. The Major rated that four-month tour, free of the racial problems that confronted him in America, as the most successful and enjoyable of his career.

In 1904 it was a different story when Taylor returned for a second tour. McIntosh also invited along two intensely racist white Americans, Floyd MacFarland and his young protégé, Iver Lawson. Iver was highly talented and would win the World Championship six months later in London. MacFarland was a truly great rider who not only won over 400 races in his career but, as a promoter and manager of several national and world champions, was one of the dominant influences on American and international cycle tracks for over two decades.

Taylor, Lawson and MacFarland were no strangers to one another; they had tangled before, and proved to be a highly volatile combination. In 1904 they produced the single most amazing and controversial series of cycle races in the history of Australia, and possibly in any country. For Major Taylor it was the worst season he ever experienced as the trio fought out racially charged battles on the cycle tracks of White Australia. Taylor had possibly the most severe fall and injury of his career, essentially suffered a nervous breakdown at the end of the tour, did not race at all for the next three years, and did not compete again in America for six years, in the twilight of his career.

The net result was that Major Taylor effectively vanished from the American sports scene. In 1932 he died destitute in a charity ward, his body unclaimed for over a week.

Prelude to Australia

In the 1890s the bicycle was a worldwide craze and tens of millions were manufactured. Except for a train on rails the machine was the fastest form of transport on the face of the earth for a brief period, a fact largely forgotten today. Bicycle racing was spectacular, exciting, glamorous, dangerous, and attracted huge crowds. For a few years it was the biggest international sport in terms of money, attendance, and following. The manufacturers and cycle race promoters invested tremendous sums in appearance and prize money, publicising events, and advertising their machines. Newspapers not only had cycling columns but some devoted entire *sections* to the bicycle and bicycle racing. It was big business.

Marshall W. 'Major' Taylor, born in 1878, got his nickname from wearing a quasi-military uniform while performing riding stunts outside an Indianapolis bicycle shop to attract customers. Taylor's employer eventually entered him in a local race against white riders as something of a joke, but the Major proved to be far more than a stunt rider. He not only won but was soon setting sprint records. Louis 'Birdie' Munger, white, and a former high wheeler cycle racer, recognised Taylor's potential. He employed him and became his mentor. When racial problems made it increasingly difficult for Taylor to train and race in the Midwest, Munger moved to Massachusetts where more liberal attitudes enabled the Major to compete regularly against white riders. Taylor's development was rapid and remarkable.

The black teenager burst on to the world cycling scene in a

spectacular manner. In his professional debut at Madison Square Garden in 1896, Taylor defeated Eddie 'Cannon' Bald, the reigning US champion. There was no mistaking the message or the messenger. In 1899, under the management of Billy Brady, a theatrical producer who also managed world boxing champion James Jeffries, Taylor won 21 of 45 races, came in second or third in the remainder, and won the World Sprint Championship in Montreal. US sports writers had proclaimed him America's cycling sprint champion in 1898. He was accorded the accolade again in 1899 and crowned official champion in 1900. (The existence of rival cycling bodies led to disputed 'national champion' claims until that year.) In 1901 Taylor went to Europe, beat the leading Continental riders, and was hailed as 'the fastest bicycle rider in the world'. They labelled him 'The Ebony Streak'.

That ebony streak, however, created problems for him. When the Major broke the racial barrier in professional bicycle racing it was at a price. He was banned from riding on southern tracks and many northern ones and subjected to racial slurs, on and off track. Finding a hotel that would take him in during his travels, or a restaurant near the velodromes that would serve him, was a constant problem, his fame notwithstanding. He was physically threatened by some of his white opponents and on the track many teamed up to try and prevent him from winning races.

However, Taylor had two particular assets. One was a phenomenally strong and resilient character. He could not have accomplished what he did, in his day, without it. Second, because of his combination of ability and colour, wherever he went he consistently attracted larger crowds than any other cyclist in the world. If the Major made an appearance at a meet the promoter was essentially guaranteed financial success. He was big business in his own right. Understandably, for one and a half decades Taylor featured prominently on international cycle tracks.

Australia was no exception. In 1902 a Sydney syndicate offered the Major £1,500 if he would race Down Under for just three months, more than 8 years of an average Australian wage earner's income. (Henceforth £ and $ refer to Australian currency unless otherwise noted.) As well, he would receive additional local appearance money and keep all prize money that he won. This last fact was particularly attractive because the promoters had conceived The Sydney Thousand, the richest cycle race in the world. An added incentive for Taylor was that he would be riding during the Australian summer (January, February and March), the winter off-season in the northern hemisphere. It was a very lucrative way to keep in training. The Major accepted the invitation

In late November, 1902, Taylor and his wife of several months, Daisy, boarded the steamer *SS Ventura* in San Francisco, bound for Sydney. While on board he first heard of the 'White Australia Policy'. It caused him great concern during the voyage.

Australia, approximately the size of the contiguous United States, and with only 3,850,000 people in 1902, had been settled by the English just 114 years before, in 1788. When they arrived they found approximately 750,000 Aboriginal inhabitants. These were dealt with in a similar manner to native Americans in the United States. By 1876 the last full-blooded Aborigine had been exterminated on the island state of Tasmania and the remaining mainland Aborigines were little more than outcasts on European-owned land.

Then, late in the 19th century, some Australian employers brought in Melanesians from several Pacific islands to work in tropical northern Australia, particularly to cut sugar cane. They were indentured, contract labour and were not intended as permanent residents. Nonetheless, many white Australians protested the importation of black foreign workers under any circumstances. It was partly a matter of protecting their jobs but there was also a strong element of

Sheet music cover page for White Australia *march*

racism. By the time the Major sailed for Australia the federal *Immigration Restriction Act 1901* had been passed, requiring all imported black workers to be removed from the country, and no more were allowed in. With few exceptions, the only dark-skinned people left in Australia were the remnants of the original Aboriginal inhabitants, and they did not count—they were not tallied in the federal census and could not vote.

The prevailing attitude at the time was well summarised by *The Bulletin*, the country's widely read, influential, self-proclaimed 'National Australian Newspaper'. Its masthead carried the motto 'Australia for the Australians'. If there were any doubts as to *The Bulletin*'s intention, in 1908 it altered the banner to read 'Australia for the White Man'.

The Major was travelling in that era before passports and visas. He had only to buy tickets for Australia and board the ship. There were no applications to embassies or consulates—it was another 40 years before the Australians even opened an Embassy in America. However, without a visa he had no prior guarantee that he would be granted entry to the country once he got there. Notwithstanding his fame, the Major was black and he was coming to 'White Australia'.

As he sailed into Sydney Harbour on December 22, 1902, Taylor was, by his own admission, worried. He had come to Australia with his wife on a delayed working honeymoon but now was unsure how he would be received. His experiences over the years had left him justifiably wary.

PART 1

The First Australian Tour

"Sportsman-like Treatment"

Sydney, early 20th century

1. Taylor is in Town

When the steamship passed through the Sydney Heads into what many have described as 'the most beautiful natural harbour in the world', the Major felt that the sight alone was worth the price of the voyage. As the SS Ventura sailed the seven miles up the harbor to the city it was met by an increasingly large number of craft. Many flew American flags and some individuals with megaphones shouted out greetings. The ship was met by the pilot boat. The pilot climbed aboard, accompanied by Hugh McIntosh, head of the syndicate which had organised Taylor's trip. After greeting McIntosh, Taylor settled back to be interviewed by the newspapermen who had also come along.

Thousands lined the dock to glimpse the 'Negro Wonder'. As a band welcomed him ashore with The Star Spangled Banner, the Major walked off the ship the personification of the sporting warrior come to do battle. He carried his personally designed adjustable handlebars and witch hazel, a medicinal preparation for inflammation and bruises. The crowd was fascinated. Although American blacks were occasionally crewmen on visiting ships and some came to Australia during the goldrush of the 1850s, few Australians in Major Taylor's era would have personally seen or met one. Many at dockside were taken aback by the fact that he was of such small physique. At only five feet seven inches he was described as 'rather good looking' and a 'nattily put together athlete'.

The Taylors were taken to the prestigious Metropole Hotel. This was radically different from their reception in San Francisco a

Sydney's Circular Quay, circa 1904, where the SS Ventura *docked*

few weeks earlier. There, during the course of a one-night layover, the honeymooners had been refused accommodation or a meal in numerous hotels. But in the view of Sydneysiders the Major's reputation and sporting prowess combined to make him an instant celebrity, a conquering hero, a one-man show. The Australians could not climb on the bandwagon quickly enough.

In their suite the Taylors were introduced to a number of prominent people, then escorted to Sydney Town Hall where they were met by the Lord Mayor, various officials, and sporting celebrities. They sat down to a banquet. After the Lord Mayor's welcome Percy Hunter, from the syndicate, outlined the negotiations that had led to Taylor coming to Australia, and toasts were proposed. Every-

one was pleased to have Major Taylor there, 'even though he should sweep over the land like a whirlwind'. It was felt that the Australian riders would profit by the experience and that the sport would be given a new impetus in the country. The Major responded with a well-received speech.

Taylor was made a member of the local YMCA, whose gymnasium he used for training while in Sydney. It was a far cry from the YMCA in his native Indianapolis, Indiana, where he first met what he described as that 'monster prejudice', and from which he was barred from exercising with white children. Taylor's association with the YMCA in Sydney went beyond the exercise room. He had an established reputation as a highly religious man who stood on his principles. One writer reported that he wouldn't even allow his trainer to repair his tyres on Sundays. *The Bulletin* cynically referred to him as the 'sanctimonious Taylor' but numerous other Australian papers were quick to point out that the Major never rode for the world championship in Europe because the races were held on Sundays and he refused to participate. As well, all of the Major's European match races, which normally would have been raced on the Sabbath, had to be re-scheduled on other days. As a result promoters paid him considerably smaller appearance fees; Taylor estimated his consequent losses up to that time at US$30,000 (£6,000).

The Major and his wife were a social phenomenon. They were deluged with hundreds of invitations during the course of their stay and proved 'about as difficult to catch unengaged as a Royal Highness'.

Sydney's George Street, showing the Town Hall, with clock tower, and domed Queen Victoria Building beyond

The 'Dark Evangelist', a member of a Worcester, Massachusetts, coloured Baptist congregation, was a popular speaker at Down Under churches. Numerous Sydney residents suddenly experienced an uncommon religious craving and the pews overflowed when Taylor appeared. *The New South Wales Baptist*, previously criticised for printing sporting news about the local Baptist Cricket Association, devoted five columns to an interview with him. The Taylors were an unqualified social success, but when the Major began training he greatly curtailed his off-track activities.

❖ ❖ ❖

Major Taylor's trip was sponsored by a syndicate led by 28-year-old Hugh D. McIntosh, a native Sydneysider. McIntosh was slightly stooped, short, thickset and muscular. He was shrewd, observant and street-wise, skills honed in his youth. Before he was ten years old he had left his widowed mother to wander about the country, undertaking an astounding array of jobs, many involving heavy physical work in difficult conditions, including labouring at the Broken Hill mines. Interspersed with his travels, he spent time back in Sydney working as a medical assistant and bath house attendant, among other things. In his mid-late teens he took up boxing under Larry Foley, who helped develop Bob Fitzsimmons and Peter Jackson. Those pugilistic skills, combined with his self-assuredness and strength, enabled him to handle with confidence a fascinating array of highly talented and sometimes intimidating athletes.

The Bulletin's *'Sanctimonious Taylor'*

Hugh developed into a man of diverse talents, tastes, and temperament, combined with intense energy and enthusiasm. With his blue eyes, close-cropped moustache, and open, attractive personality he forged his way in society. He collected fine books and used coarse language; donated to charities but was unscrupulous in business; was a life member of the Royal Australian Historical Society and yet was not averse to a 'stoush', or fight. *The Melbourne Punch* characterised him as a hustler, among many of his activities 'commercial and concupiscent adventures', a loyal wife notwithstanding.

But above all, as Frank Van Straten, his biographer, effectively chronicles, Hugh was Australia's first great entrepreneur. McIntosh would gain international recognition in 1908 by promoting the first

Hugh D. McIntosh

black–white heavyweight boxing championship match between Jack Johnson and Tommy Burns and filming it for overseas showing. That was the year he also acquired the nickname 'Huge Deal' McIntosh, a source of pride the rest of his life. New South Wales Premier Jack Lang called him a 'supershowman if ever there was one … the Barnum of Australia'. He went on to become a major international player in boxing and theatrical circles in America and the United Kingdom, and a wealthy man of influence and power, who knew how to use and abuse it. John Hetherington, a friend, called him 'an unrepentant buccaneer'; in his 1981 book, Keith Dunstan, a Melbourne writer, labelled McIntosh a 'ratbag'.

McIntosh achieved early financial stability by marketing that quintessentially Australian item, the meat pie, at sporting fixtures, and developing a solid catering business. Among the popular outlets for his products were cycle tracks. There he saw opportunity, and no one proved quicker at grasping it than Hugh.

McIntosh, who had raced briefly in 1900–1901 to less than stellar accolades, realised that the money was in the promotion and management. There had long been tremendous tension and internecine rivalry between many cycling clubs, their officers, and the governing bodies. McIntosh set about consolidating his position in that administrative maelstrom. He founded one club, became a member of a number of others, was elected as an officer in several, and in 1901 was appointed a member of the Council of the League of Wheelmen, the overall governing body. He manoeuvred himself into the position of General Secretary, from which he exercised tremendous power for several years.

For Taylor's visit, McIntosh and several others formed the Sydney syndicate referred to variously as the Sydney Summer Nights Amusement Committee, or Summer Nights Amusements. Among its members were George Wynne, a writer with *The Daily Telegraph*, a leading Sydney newspaper; Paddy O'Brien, an official in the New South Wales League of Wheelmen; Percy Hunter, another journalist, and President of the venerable Australian Bicycle Club; and Tom Scott. The latter two were appointed Major Taylor's official managers during his tour. The group had strong influence with *The Daily Telegraph*, which they used to great advantage for publicity purposes.

After McIntosh created his commercial cycle racing syndicate there were complaints that a number of the League's decisions and activities were tailored to his Amusements Committee's commercial benefit. The Committee's subsequent manipulations of cycling activities led to them being referred to by the *Gunnedah Advertiser* as 'a school of sharks'.

*The Metropole Hotel,
the Taylors' residence
while in Sydney*

Major Taylor's fame, abilities, religious principles and curiosity value combined to make him a very marketable commodity and, for the syndicate, a highly profitable one. He needed to be. He had just cost the Sydney Summer Nights Amusement Committee more money than any other cyclist in the world. They contracted to pay him £1,500 ($525,000 today) for 16 appearances in Australia.

Taylor's fame and high price must be put in perspective. In the United States in 1902 professional sports involved neither the range nor scale of activities of today. Professional football was minor, the National Football League not yet formed. Basketball had only been invented a few years before and was still finding its feet. There was no professional tennis. Horse racing could be lucrative for breeders and owners but the jockeys themselves earned relatively little. Only a handful of top-level boxers could make good money, and only then in some fights. Baseball was a notable exception. By 1902 a few (but not many) well-established ball players were earning between US$3,000 and US$5,000 per year, which was five to ten times as much as the average American worker received.

The really big money, both in America and abroad, was in cycling, which was in its own league when it came to participant earnings. For nearly two decades it offered greater rewards for a greater number of talented athletes than any other arena.

With the invention of the safety bicycle in 1885 and the commercial manufacture of pneumatic tyres in 1888, the public was handed its greatest personal transport advance in history. The machine's impact was immense and wide-ranging. By the mid-1890s bicycles were relatively cheap as American and European manufacturers shipped millions of them around the world. Large numbers were bought on hire purchase (or time payment, as it is known in America) and along with sewing machines were a major element in popularising that financial concept with consumers. The remarkable device was light, strong, easy to maintain, could be stored on a porch or indoors, and could be readily ridden 70–100 miles in a day. In exploiting that capability, cycle tourists created the forerunners of the automobile clubs in America, England, Europe and Australia and developed the modern road map. Such widespread personal transport freedom had never existed before, in either rural or urban areas.

In the sporting world the crucial fact was that the man-machine combination was fast. From a standing start a man could outsprint a cyclist for about a hundred yards, but beyond that the cyclist would quickly pull away. A horse could beat a pedaller for about two miles but ultimately the bicyclist was far faster and more durable. By 1898 a solo cyclist had ridden 428 miles in only 24 hours. No horse and rider could remotely match that. In 1899 'Mile-a-Minute' Murphy pedalled 60 miles per hour behind a train on a special board track laid between the rails. Many did not believe it initially.

Hence, by the early 1890s all the elements were there to support a major new international sporting industry. And support it they did, on an immense scale. The sporting aspects of the bicycle were quickly developed and basic competitive and commercial patterns established that would be adopted for motor racing in just a few years. Huge amounts of prize money were offered by promoters. The manufacturers sponsored riders, teams, and events and bought endorsements. Since anyone could walk into a local cycle shop and buy the exact models used on the tracks, right down to the tyres, manufacturers poured immense funds into cycle racing, each trying to convince the everyday rider that its machine or tyre was the best. Aspiring champions were able to test themselves against their friends on the road. If things looked promising they needed only to join a club and begin competing. Within a few years the widespread popularity of the machine created a vast audience, its members enthused by the daily excitement and newfound freedom of being able to go so far, so fast.

Bicycle racing thus must be appreciated for what it was—for over a decade the predominant international sport, creating great public excitement on and off track. The accomplishments of the top riders, and above all Major Taylor, were followed in detail in newspapers and magazines around the world. No other sport had such extensive and consistent international coverage. It was a phenomenon that both portended and laid the groundwork for many changes in professional sports.

That phenomenon can be no better measured than by the amount of money involved. Relative amounts have already been noted with respect to Major Taylor and Tiger Woods. In addition to the £4,000 pounds earned by Taylor in Australia in early 1903, he garnered another £6,000 during the following European summer. That brought his total for the year to some £10,000 ($3,500,000 in 2009 Australian equivalent wages). While he had to pay his own travel and accommodation costs, and support his trainer, he was still left with a remarkable amount of money. Furthermore, he got to keep it—there was no personal income tax until 1913. His religious principles take on added significance in light of the above; Taylor's own estimated lost appearance money of £6,000, from refusing to ride on Sunday, represents $2,100,000 in 2009 Australian equivalent wages.

Despite Taylor's high Australian tour fee the promoters had grounds for believing that they would do well out of the arrangement. Taylor's ability to attract immense crowds at American and European tracks was an established fact. His sprinting speed, his world records, and his defeat of all the major American and European champions in man-to-man match races would seem to assure huge crowds in Australia as well. As a precedent, the legendary American cyclist Arthur 'Zimmy' Zimmerman had toured Australia nine years before. In two appearances in Sydney he drew 60,000 spectators. Yet Taylor was a far faster sprinter than Zimmerman ever was, and from the promoters' perspective there was an even more attractive aspect: Zimmy had ridden in only one race per meet but Taylor had agreed to ride in several races in each of his 16 meet appearances. That would add to his drawing power.

Newspaper reports indicate that the average attendance was usually close to 20,000, sometimes less, on occasion more. The admission charge was one shilling per person, or £1,000 per meet. Allowing £500 per meet for expenses (prize money, ground rental, advertising, officials, and so on, though an exact figure is not known), they stood to net £500. For 16 meets that represents £8,000 or $2,800,000 in 2009 equivalent wage earnings. However, the profits were almost certainly *much* more than that since thousands of fans paid an additional shilling at each meet to sit in the grandstands and there was income from concessions (McIntosh operated his own catering service in New South Wales). Clearly, the investment in Taylor was a risk well worth taking and demonstrates the importance of the black rider on the international circuit. Both as athlete and celebrity Major Taylor was a 'superstar' long before the term was invented.

The promoters had read the mind of the Australian public superbly. Cycle racing had a solid base. The League of Wheelmen, the governing body for all racing in New South Wales, had a record 71 clubs with 10,000 enrolled members and had issued 1,250 racing licences. Although public attendance at the big meets had been on the decline for some years, Taylor's arrival on the scene reversed that trend strikingly. *The Sydney Morning Herald* and *The Daily Telegraph* gave extensive coverage to Major Taylor, the latter moving much of its reportage from the sports pages to the news pages and, in conjunction with Taylor's opening appearances in Sydney, featuring a large montage of photographs in the paper. As the Melbourne *Argus* put it, 'Cycling is in and all other sports must take a back seat'. Given all the factors surrounding his tour it is not surprising that McIntosh had assured there was no colour bar at dockside the day Taylor arrived.

The banquets, welcomings, church appearances and interviews were peripheral. The Major had come to ride. Immediately he asked to see the 'great battlefield—the bicycle track'. The importance

"Blessed are the Pacemakers", from The Bulletin

of cycle racing in that era is evidenced by the fact that a cycle track was built around the hallowed Sydney Cricket Ground in 1896, and two years later lights were installed as well, to make night racing possible. When they took Major Taylor out to see it for the first time, he received an unwelcome surprise. Cricket fields are oval and, as is the way with ovals, there is no straightaway. The concrete SCG cycle track had two reasonably sharp banked curves on each end, with two long gentle curves between. Also the track was a third of a mile around. Thus Taylor had to learn to adapt to a three-lap mile, ridden entirely on a continuing left-hand curve. It caused him, in his own words, 'considerable annoyance' until he adjusted to it. No one else ever seemed to notice it being a problem for him.

Buchet motor cycle, typical of pacing machines of the era

Any possible doubts as to the Major's ability to revive interest in cycling were put to rest on his first day of training. At the Sydney Cricket Ground, on the hottest day of the summer so far, he appeared wearing black tights and a pale blue singlet (he admitted he was vain about his appearance). Three thousand spectators applauded him as he pedalled onto the track at 6:10 pm. Over the next several weeks large crowds attended every session.

His famous physique was analysed closely. The general consensus was that he was 'a very evenly made, well-turned, manly fellow'. *The Bulletin* referred to his bulging calves, but *The Worker* took *The Bulletin* to task for its inaccurate description. In contrast to most cyclists, *The Worker* noted, Taylor's calves were not particularly bulging, but in fact were lightly and symmetrically built. The Major was clearly a physical specimen par excellence, 'beautifully proportioned and a mass of muscle'. He was a champion, 'every inch of him'.

Taylor won over the crowds and the Australian cyclists with his geniality and generosity. What particularly surprised the local riders was the Major's willingness to train with them, side by side. They had expected him to do much of his work in secret. Contrary to all expectations he unhesitatingly displayed his Massey-Harris bicycle and allowed them to size it up for themselves—the gearing, the cranks, the frame, and the pedal reach. These were commonly considered secrets in the trade. Of considerable interest were his adjustable handlebars. They were new to the country, and for decades afterward Australian cyclists commonly referred to adjustable ones as 'Major Taylors'.

Above all, the Australians were astonished at the tremendous amount of work he did in his twice-a-day training program. In particular he spent much of his time riding behind two motorcycle pacers. Although the machines had been demonstrated on Australian tracks, Major Taylor was the first cyclist in the country to use them regularly. They were noisy, exciting, fast, and a factor in the crowds regularly coming out to watch the Major's sessions.

Taylor was also pleased when he found that there would be no 'colour line'. It removed a great pressure and allowed him to go about his physical preparations mentally unhampered. Taylor's managers

*Taylor with his
Australian trainer,
Sid Melville*

appointed Sid Melville as his trainer. Throughout the tour and the
one the following year Sid proved to be 'one of the most faithful and
loyal trainers a man could have'. During that balmy early summer
Taylor got down to business.

Strategy, tactics and riding styles were of particular concern
for both the Major and his rivals. The Australians were fascinated by

Taylor. He rode low on the bicycle and onlookers were amused by his habit of watching the riders close behind him by a slight, unusual turn of the head; it gave him a 'comic' appearance. While a number of observers thought Taylor might not gain his form quickly in the reversed seasons it was generally acknowledged that with his greater experience he had 'headwork superiority'.

Major Taylor and Don Walker

Taylor watched his opponents carefully. The Australian riders had already been racing for two months and were in top form. As a group they were very fast but the Major did not rate them equal to the

really high-class individual sprinters he had encountered in Europe and America. Never having seen them before, however, he had to be wary and learn their nuances.

Of all the Australian riders, one stood out: Don Walker. He had come to Australia from Canada in 1879 at the age of five. During Zimmerman's tour of Australia in the mid-1890s Walker was one of only three riders to defeat him. By 1899, Don had placed in the top three of the Australian Championships for 12 years. When the Major met him, Walker was the current Australian Champion, held many records, and was at his peak. Taylor developed great respect for Don's talents and after his racing days were over ranked him as one of the ten best foreign riders he faced. Coming from the Major, who over one and a half decades raced against every European and American champion, that was high praise indeed. Walker was very popular, extremely likable and greatly respected. He 'took a fancy' to the Major, whom he felt was 'a nice, decent fellow with no brag'. Taylor and the unassuming Australian became 'fast chums'.

But goodwill and training were not the primary objectives of Taylor's tour. He was there to race. His first meet was scheduled less than two weeks after stepping ashore in Sydney. The Major knew that he was not yet in perfect condition but he was ready. Australian observers said that he had trained until he looked 'all wire'. As had become obvious, he was possessed with an 'ever-working brain and was as quick as a cat'. The Australians saw it all come together for the first time on the Sydney Cricket Ground on January 3, 1903.

PLAN OF TRACK, SHOWING THE POSITIONS OF THE RIDERS IN THE
FINISH OF THE INTERNATIONAL CHAMPIONSHIP.

*Sydney Cricket
Ground layout,
1903*

20

2. The Worcester Whirlwind

Sydneysiders called it 'The Major Taylor Carnival'. Numerous articles about him appeared in newspapers, magazines, and journals. Advertisers cashed in on the hoopla. A Sydney haberdasher placed a cartoon in *The Sunday Times* showing himself on a bicycle, as the city's 'Major Tailor', leading his competitors. While Sydney's *Worker* took umbrage at the extensive coverage, in particular accusing *The Daily Telegraph* of 'booming the show' for the sponsoring syndicate, few others appeared to care. They were too busy enjoying all those bicycle meets featuring the 'Black Cyclone'.

On the Saturday morning of Taylor's Australian debut people began streaming toward Moore Park on the extra trams that had been provided for the event. Those running from Elizabeth Street and Central Railway disembarked passengers directly at the Driver Avenue entrance to the SCG. By early afternoon over 20,000 people were at the Sydney Cricket Ground, the largest number to attend a cycle race since Zimmerman's tour in bicycling's heyday. When Taylor emerged on to the circuit he was greeted with a welcoming cheer. A few minutes later Don Walker appeared to an equally rousing ovation. The pair, along with the other competitors, pedalled around the track, warming up. The one-third mile oval concrete track was about 40 feet wide, and banked to nearly 35 degrees on the two sharp curves.

The big event of the day was the Quarter Mile International Championship, less than a lap. Major Taylor and Don Walker were pitted against each other and another notable rider, Bob Lewis, former Australian mile record holder and among the fastest sprinters in the country.

The riders finally lined up and the crowd tensed in anticipation. The starter's gun fired, sending them on their way. The pace was relatively slow through the first curve and around the back sweep. Into the second and final curve Lewis held the lead, with Taylor and Walker immediately behind. Suddenly, with 200 yards to go, Lewis made his bid and sprinted forward. Simultaneously he felt a momentary sensation, as if he had a puncture. Taylor had inadvertently bumped his wheel, a potentially dangerous situation. Walker, seeing the incident, swiftly moved away, thinking that the Major was going to crash to the ground alongside him. However, Taylor made such an extraordinary recovery that he not only kept up, but 'scarcely swerved from his track'.

Then the Major executed his spectacular jump.

As one journalist described it, when the time comes for him to move he 'fairly shakes up his wheel, lifts it along through the air, as it were, and jumps past his competitors'. Taylor applied so much power that he sometimes lost momentary traction with his rear wheel. The net effect, as Lewis commented afterward, was that 'suddenly something flashed past me. Then I gave up thinking I could win'. Lewis could hardly believe it. Before he knew what had happened, the Major was two lengths ahead. Don Walker, alongside Taylor, was taken totally by surprise: 'The quickness with which he made his famous jump was absolutely a revelation to me'. Neither Australian had a remote chance of catching him. To the roar of the crowd Taylor swept over the finish line the victor. Lewis, who only moments before thought that he might actually win, found himself in third place as Walker, recovering, powered past him at the finish line.

The crowd cheered the American wildly as he began his victory lap. Then, according to *all* newspaper accounts, the spectators were stunned into silence by what happened next.

Major Taylor pulled out an American flag and held it at arm's length in the breeze as he rode around the track. It had never been

done before in Australia. The deafening applause from the multitude 'stopped short' as many thought that Taylor was 'crowing' over his victory. As the Major later explained, he thought it appropriate to show the flag in an international cycling meet. But he quickly found out that kind of display was not customary in Australia. Aussies did not emulate the Yankee penchant for flag waving. As *The Sydney Mail* commented, 'the idea was no doubt harmless, but it was new to Australian sportsmen and required some thinking over'. Taylor was completely forgiven as soon as the Australians came to realise that it was simply a cross-cultural misunderstanding. The Major, 'one of the most modest and retiring of men', felt 'pained' that he was seen to be lauding it over a defeated adversary. He never did it again.

Taylor winning in Sydney

The final event of the day, once more featuring Major Taylor and Don Walker, was the five-mile. Taylor doubted his fitness for it, but agreed to go ahead for the sake of the crowd. The race had a first-class field and was fast from the start. On the fifteenth and final lap, on the back stretch, Taylor was sitting in third place behind Arthur Gudgeon and Dick Mutton. Immediately behind rode Lewis and Walker. As the riders swept around the final banked turn Don pulled out wide and shot past all four into the lead. The crowd screamed relentlessly as the quintet dashed for the finish line. Walker crossed a length ahead, having set an Australian quarter-mile sprint record in the final lap. Gudgeon and Mutton dead heated behind and Taylor was a close fourth. Wave after wave of cheers swept around the ground as Walker rode his victory lap. The Major pulled alongside and they continued around a second time, shaking hands. The spectators 'climbed on their seats and cheered anew'.

In subsequent interviews the Major commended Gudgeon and Mutton and reinforced his opinion of Don Walker. He concluded that Australian riders were much better than was generally appreciated overseas. For their part the Australians acknowledged that they had not seen Taylor at his best in the five-mile. As Walker summarised it, 'Which of us Australian riders could have put up such a sprint in the Quarter-mile Race, and then have gone through a five-mile race, in which the last quarter was run in Australian record time, and finish right on the line with the winners after being off the boat only a fortnight after a long sea voyage?' It was a golden day in Australian–American sporting relations.

❖ ❖ ❖

Cycle racing, like all sporting activities, has its own particular atmosphere. Among the riders the nervous tension before the race start is palpable. Some fidget; others are quiet but tense; a few are talkative, even agitated; some are so hyped that they fly off the handle if spoken to. As they roll to the line there are anxious inspections of equipment, a quick spin of a wheel, the brushing of tyres with hands, and the tightening of toestraps. Muscles are alternately relaxed and flexed, and the riders inhale deeply.

When the gun fires the first 50 yards can be agonising as the air sucked in burns the back of the dry throat. The race effort can be intensely painful or, more rarely when super fit, a rider can experience a silky, fluid leg motion without any seeming strain. In the affray racers can hear the fine 'zip' of an accelerating tyre, smell the sweat and balm in the middle of a bunch, hear the curses as riders switch or come too close, be mesmerised by the spinning wheel in front, and be surprised by the unexpected wisecrack during an intense struggle.

The journalists of the era reported extensively on the technicalities of the races and the roars of the crowds, but only infrequently on the emotional aspects. Nonetheless, for every rider, every race was a physical, emotional and mental strain. The cyclists were not automatons rolling about a track, but human beings doing battle with one another in a dangerous sport. Serious injuries were common, and death an occasional fact. The competitors were laying their physical ability and competitive–emotional competence open to the intense scrutiny of the crowds, their competitors, and themselves. It could be a cruel judgment.

❖ ❖ ❖

Throughout January the interest remained intense and the cycling exciting. On the Monday following the Major's debut 15,000 watched him set a world record in a preliminary half-mile heat. In a subsequent heat two riders fell spreadeagled on the track while a third was thrown against an overhead electric light support and suffered painful groin and back injuries. Taylor, swerving to avoid the crash, was beaten by Larry Corbett from New South Wales, who needed no

Cycling carnival at night, Sydney Cricket Ground

excuse for his victory; he tied the world record for the distance, which the Major had set earlier in the evening. In response, Taylor took another three-fifths of a second off the record in the final. The crowd responded with thunderous applause. They were witnessing inspired riding on all sides and getting their money's worth.

The fast racing and sportsmanship continued unabated. On Wednesday, January 21st, 25,000 people showed up for the night races despite the fact that it rained from 8 o'clock on. In the Centennial

One Mile the Major set an Australian record. Later, after one rider had already fallen in the slippery conditions and broken his jaw, Taylor saw an opponent, Bob Walne, slip and fall on the track soon after the starter's gun went off. The Major immediately turned around and pedalled back to the starting line, signalling a new race. His action was appreciated and acknowledged by the crowd.

By the end of The Major Taylor Carnival it was obvious that the 'Worcester Whirlwind' was superior to his competitors. *The Worker* concluded that the Australian riders were simply not in the same class as Taylor; without doubt he was 'the greatest rider ever seen on these shores'. Likewise *The Arrow* felt that Taylor had 'settled all pretensions that an Australian rider could defeat him in a straight out contest'. *The Bulletin* was the only publication to express doubts about the Major's physical superiority. In comparing him with Don Walker it felt that Taylor merely had 'more courage and judgment'. *The Worker* replied quickly and sharply, 'which is a mighty poor compliment to the white man'. Its view was that 'colour or no colour, Taylor is the better man'. It had been a marvellous

Major and Mrs Taylor

month. At the end of January the Major and Daisy boarded a train for the state of Victoria.

❖❖❖

Melbourne's reception for the Taylors at the railway station was the equal of Sydney's dockside welcome. Two officials from the Victorian League of Wheelmen managed to reach his reserved carriage only after a great struggle. It took some time to get the couple out of the surging crowd and to their hotel. Shortly afterwards they were taken to a 'monster' public reception at the Port Phillip Club Hotel, where the Taylors were welcomed by the Lord Mayor. The Major was modest, unassuming and 'very gentlemanly in deportment'. His physical appearance was the subject of great attention. Those who expected to see 'a big brawny individual' were disappointed. Instead they saw 'what may be described as a pocket edition', of 'barely average height', but very muscular and 'sinewy'. In his speech Taylor said he hoped to be able to ride 'so as to merit all the flattering compliments'.

It was not to be. He had caught what he thought was a bad cold on the last, rainy night of the Sydney Carnival. It became worse on his journey south and after the reception he was confined to bed for two weeks with influenza. During that time—and against doctor's orders—he pedalled an exhibition lap at the Exhibition Grounds, where the stall-holders sold 'Major Taylor' peaches and apples. It was the principal bicycle-racing venue for Melbourne, and like the Sydney Cricket Ground, had a lit track. In contrast to the SCG, though, it was only a fifth of a mile around. In 1897, at the peak of the cycle craze in the country, the Australian Natives' Association Wheel Race drew a reported 35,000. Photographs suggest it was no exaggeration.

The Melbourne press took the opportunity of seeing Taylor

*Australian Natives
Association Day
Races, Melbourne
Exhibition Grounds,
late 1890s*

on a bicycle for the first time to describe him to any of their readers
who were not in attendance. One journalist, in the horse-crazy country that Australia is, likened him to a thoroughbred: 'He has blood
and his every movement is instinct with it, being highly strung, alert
and nimble'. Then the writer turned anthropologist. The Major's
skin 'shines like satin and his face smiles pleasantly under his centre-
parted, closely cropped curly hair as he walks to the starting point. He
is a typical Negro'.

Taylor's inability to race during the fortnight was a great dis-appointment. In response, the promoters arranged two special match races after he recovered. One was against Don Walker and the other against George Morgan, who achieved the honour by defeating all other riders in a series of qualifying heats.

The Taylor–Walker match was a best-of-three format, the winner receiving the entire £100 purse. In the opening half-mile race Taylor immediately manoeuvred Walker into the lead. Halfway through, Taylor suddenly jumped and his front wheel came off the track. There was a great roar from the crowd, who had finally witnessed it. The Major shot past Walker, 'who seemed to stand still' in comparison. The second race, over a mile, saw Taylor again manoeuvre Walker into the lead and then on the last lap, in virtually the same position, bunch himself 'in an extraordinary fashion, and with a spring' execute the famous jump again. The crowd was amazed at the speed and power and cheered wildly.

Several days later Taylor met George Morgan in a best-of-three match race. The first two races were easily won by the Major, who jumped Morgan in each case and walked away with the £125 prize. It had been agreed, however, that should Taylor win in two straight there would be a special mile race later in the evening, pitting all of the major contestants against one another. From the start that race was extremely fast and it picked up in intensity throughout. As they came to the bell lap, Taylor was in second place, behind Bob Walne. Another rider, Ernie Pye, who would eventually become famous in America, pulled up on the outside, boxing him in. The crowd thought he was beaten. Then, 120 yards from the finish, Major Taylor momentarily back-pedalled and fell behind Pye. Before Pye could react to slow himself, Taylor swung to the outside of him and jumped his machine. Taylor's finish, adjudged by one observer as 'one of the most marvellous sprints ever', staggered everyone present as he outraced Walne over the line by inches. The Major later said that it was the best thing he had done in Australia.

The Melbournians were dumbfounded. After two weeks of illness and only a few days of training Taylor had beaten Don Walker and George Morgan in straight heat victories, and then defeated the best riders in the country in a special mile. One reporter concluded that Major Taylor was nothing less than 'a super man on a bicycle'. He left the city in a blaze of glory.

❖ ❖ ❖

In Adelaide the Major and his wife emerged from their boudoir railway car into another huge crowd and were cheered. They were formally welcomed at the South Australia Hotel, where Taylor's 'quaint' American accent won over the locals. An Adelaide newspaper noted that 'If any coloured gentleman can claim to be a "white man", it is Major Taylor'. The clergymen in that City of Churches admired his Sabbatarian principles.

To benefit a local hospital in need all agreed that there would be an entry fee of threepence to watch him train at the Adelaide Oval. It was there that a flat, grass cycling track had been built in 1883. In 1899, a banked concrete track replaced it. Unlike Sydney and Melbourne, there was no lighting, so all meets were held during the day. During the Major's time there was only grandstand seating for about 4,000 people, so most spectators stood. Large crowds around the one-third mile perimeter cheered his training sprints.

The meet was originally thought to be a financial gamble because an England–South Australia cricket match was on over the

Taylor training behind pace at the Adelaide Oval, 1903

*Major Taylor,
after winning the
Sir Edwin Smith
Stakes, Adelaide,
1903*

same period and rain was threatening. But thousands upon thousands turned out on each of the three days of races. Among the many spectators, the English and South Australian cricketers showed up to watch the phenomenal athlete. After it was all over the South Australian League of Wheelmen had a £500 profit.

Taylor provided the most astounding riding display the city had ever seen. In 14 starts over three days he won 11 firsts and 3 seconds. He picked up £150 appearance money, £178 in stakes, and set new Australian quarter and half-mile records. 'Salvos of cheers rent the air' as Taylor circled the track with his blue ribbon, presented by Lady Smith for winning the Sir Edwin Smith Stakes. A large crowd gathered around the Major for his victory photograph. The Major loved Adelaide, Adelaide loved the Major, and between them they put on the greatest cycling carnival ever witnessed in the city.

❖ ❖ ❖

Major Taylor made his last Australian appearance in Victoria. There, on April 13th, he won the International Five Mile Championship. It was the culmination to a spectacular season on the track. He had earlier won the Quarter Mile Championship (in Sydney) and the International One Mile championship (in Adelaide).

The four month-tour was a financial success for Taylor but personally, it was even more satisfying. As the Major summed it up, Australians had welcomed him with a warmth, enthusiasm and spirit unlike anything he had ever known. In view of the fact that he had arrived in the country with 'dire misgivings' with respect to the colour issue, he received more pleasure from the tour than any other in his racing career.

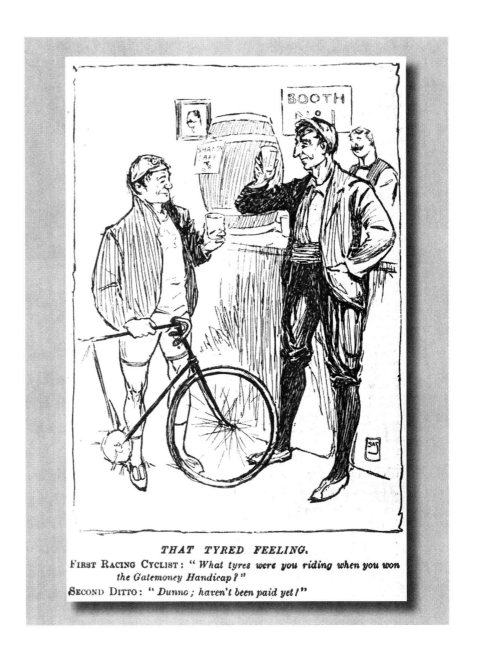

THAT TYRED FEELING.

FIRST RACING CYCLIST : "*What tyres were you riding when you won the Gatemoney Handicap ?*"

SECOND DITTO : "*Dunno ; haven't been paid yet !*"

The Bulletin's *comment on the integrity of racing cyclists*

3. The Fringes of Honesty

That 1903 Down Under summer could almost have been called golden for Taylor. But not quite. The glory, the goodwill, the sportsmanship and the friendliness throughout the tour were ultimately overshadowed at the end by one ominous fact: Major Taylor did not even qualify for the final of The Sydney Thousand, the world's richest cycle race. The surrounding circumstances deeply disturbed many in the country, including Taylor himself. As *The Sydney Sportsman* wrote, 'there must be something in the sport of cycling that insensibly leads to crookedness'. There was. Money.

Professional bicycle racing in Australia in 1903, as in other times and places, was about making money. The Major had great talent and appeal and made the most by far. While the Australian riders benefitted from studying his training techniques, analysing his tactics and strategy, and emulating him to the extent they could, Taylor's dominance meant that relatively little prize money found its way into anyone else's bank account. Not surprisingly, as the season progressed a number of riders began thinking about rectifying the situation, by whatever means.

Five basic factors were involved in the racing that year: wind resistance, large prize money, betting, the Major's superior riding skills, and handicap racing. These can be combined in a number of remarkably complex ways, and the Australians had considerable experience at it.

Wind resistance is the fundamental element that cycle racers must combat. At full racing speed some 90 per cent of riding effort is absorbed in overcoming it. Anything that can reduce that burden is sought after. Modern cyclists use streamlined helmets, slippery clothing, shaven legs, specially shaped spokes, solid wheels—anything that will lessen friction against the body and machine and smooth the flow of air around both.

In Major Taylor's day there were (and still are) three approaches to overcoming wind resistance. One was simply to ride as low as possible on the bicycle and decrease the frontal area. To that end had the Major developed his adjustable handlebar that slid along an extended gooseneck and allowed him to lean further forward than other riders.

The second method was to ride so slowly that wind resistance was not a significant factor most of the time. In a mile race, for example, the cyclists might pedal the first three quarters of it of very slowly, sprinting only the last few hundred yards.

The third tactic to overcoming wind resistance was to share the burden by taking turns in the lead. As it was to everyone's mutual benefit, it was common practice. Typically, after a given distance the front rider moved out wide, allowing the other(s) to go underneath, and pulled back in at the tail. Toward the finish of the race, of course, it became every man for himself.

In terms of money, there was a lot at stake for the riders that summer in Australia. The winners of the Austral Wheel, the Westral Wheel, and The Sydney Thousand would collect from £400 to £750 each, and the other place-getters up to £100. The typical first prize for the other major races in which Taylor rode was £100–£125. Winners of qualifying heats commonly won £1–£5. As well, there was additional money for setting a record, and in some races a bonus for the leader of each lap. Thus, a rider of lesser ability, knowing he had little chance of winning, could still pick up a tidy amount by riding hard in the earlier going.

There was even more at stake off track, because gambling

was rampant. Although it was technically illegal to bet at most cycling venues, Australian society, police, and officials generally overlooked it. While many opposed any wagering, others had long accepted the dictum that 'betting is the life and soul of any sport'. Despite the speed and excitement of bicycle racing, some felt that 'unless one has his little bit on the man of his choice, one cannot raise three ha'porth of enthusiasm over such a race'. Unfortunately the racing was not always a model of purity. There were continued complaints about the blatantly 'stiff', 'dead', 'cronk', and 'crook' riding. Some suggested that cycling officials should take more notice of such matters; others pointed out that the officials themselves were too busy doing business with the bookies.

Bookmakers, such as these at the Kalgoorlie, W.A. racetrack in 1904, also worked the lucrative Westral Wheel cycle races

In Europe and North America most major cycle races were 'scratch' races. That is, everyone started from the same point. Handicap races tended to be reserved only for second-rate riders and in-

volved relatively small prize money. In Australia, in contrast, handicap racing was more popular than anywhere else in the world, and was the format used in most major races. It was a peculiar feature Down Under, which was commented upon by numerous foreigners.

The logic of handicap racing is quite simple. If one rider is markedly superior to all others, and all start from the same spot at the same time, the markedly superior rider will finish first every time, other things being equal. It may be a true reflection of the riders' talents, but it makes for 'bloody boring racing'. For those interested in betting it is an unmitigated disaster; everyone knows what the result will probably be. In handicap racing, in contrast, the slower riders are given head starts, the amount depending upon their previous racing performances and general ability. The handicaps can vary radically. During Major Taylor's tour, for example, in a one-mile race the riders in front of him typically had head starts ranging anywhere from 10 yards to 200 yards. Ideally, if the handicappers had done their job properly and the riders rode to form, all of the racers would come across the finish line more or less at the same time. The net result would be an extremely exciting finish, satisfying racing for the riders, and a great betting atmosphere. In theory.

In reality, however, handicap racing, like all bicycle racing, suffered from the problem of wind resistance. As a consequence, riders who were particularly close to one another when the gun sounded would quickly bunch up and pace one another throughout the race. What generally resulted was that those near the back mark (the starting line) would tend to form a 'back bunch' and those further down the track, the 'front markers', would tend to form a 'front bunch'. The back markers paced one another in their attempt to close the gap with the front markers. Meanwhile, the front markers simply raced for the finish line as fast as possible.

Australian riders had long accepted the concept of 'teaming' or 'combinations' in handicap races. That is, deliberate pre-race arrangements were made among the riders to form specific groups. Furthermore, within each group they often decided who would be paced to victory and the winner would share his prize money equally with the other riders in his bunch. It became, in essence, a race between two groups.

Major Taylor complicated matters because he refused to make arrangements with anyone. His reputation as a man of high principle preceded him to Australia. As *The Advertiser* wrote, 'He always rides to win. He never sells a race'. With his ability he could quickly catch up with the back bunch, assist them to catch the front bunch, and then sprint ahead of everyone at the finish to collect the prize money. In the final analysis the Australian back markers were essentially helping Taylor set himself up for victory. Understandably many of them did not appreciate it. *The Sydney Sportsman* summarised it well: 'The course of the season could not have proceeded more pleasantly than it did until it dawned on the "bullockers" of the bike that they were cycling for coppers while Taylor was getting the gold'. From that time on, it noted, Taylor's track trips became increasingly difficult.

If Australia's top riders expected to win much money they had to figure out some way to stop the Major. As Don Walker said, 'No Australian has a show with Major Taylor—not unassisted, but it is wonderful what a scheming combination can accomplish'. And that's what the Major ultimately confronted—combinations formed specifically to defeat him. When discussing the skill of Australian riders in handicap racing Taylor said they 'have no superiors in the world in this respect', and were as game as anyone he ever competed against. He eventually discovered that the Aussies could play a very mean game indeed.

Some believed that if Taylor were given a sufficiently large handicap, it might prove very difficult for him to win races. Indeed, on his very first appearance Down Under he was lined up not at the start line, but five yards *behind* it—the first time in Australian cycling history that it happened. However, throughout the season Taylor would quickly close the short gap to the next riders who, being Australia's best, themselves started only slightly ahead of him, and they quickly formed a fast back bunch.

Ultimately it boiled down to a simple fact. Major Taylor had to be prevented from catching up with the front bunch or, once he was with the front bunch, he had to be 'pocketed' or 'boxed in' such that he could not break free at the finish. Neither of the tactics was team racing in the original Australian sense. They were outright attempts to defeat one man, to others' benefit. As one writer commented, 'No one will ride in Taylor's interests for nothing. Those who pace him should expect remuneration'. Since he would not remunerate them, they were not keen to pace him. One local cyclist summed it up for his countrymen: 'Taylor was paid handsomely for coming to Australia, and they were under no obligation to assist him to win'.

As the riders intensified their efforts through the season to defeat Taylor it became obvious to the crowds that there were unfair combinations in operation and they did not like it. In his popularity the Major had attracted a class of patrons to the track who had not come for a long time, if ever, and were not aware of some of the riding schemes. To them it looked 'dark and deceitful'. Much of it was.

Major Taylor felt that there was no just basis upon which to assess handicaps so that they accurately tested one rider's ability over another. After much experience with it he concluded that handicap racing only 'caused a lot of scheming and crookedness'. In particular, it was open to gross corruption. On the track there were innumerable opportunities and possibilities for double-crossing. For example, a team of back markers might be sold out by one of its members who would secretly agree with the front markers not to assist the back bunch to catch up. And vice versa, ad infinitum.

Officials at the Sydney Thousand, 1903, including Honourary Surgeons, Drs Muskett (left), and Gledden, seated

Off track, when betting, the riders were in an advantageous position through knowing what teams had been formed, and who was the chosen 'winner' from either or both bunches. Rather than having to wager on an entire field, they were effectively only betting on which of the two teams would come in first. In the extreme, all the riders would agree between themselves—or be told by outside influences—who the victor would be, share the prize money equally, and lay massive side bets. Just such a scheme was at the centre of a national controversy in the 1901 Austral Wheel Race, Australia's most prestigious and richest at the time.

To make matters worse there was one fundamental fact about handicap racing that perpetually threatened all schemes and team arrangements, honest or dishonest: some riders would deliberately perform below their ability over a several week period leading up to a lucrative race, so as to receive a large handicap. On the day of the big event they would then turn in an 'outstanding' performance to finish among the prize-winners, in the process upsetting other competitors, in both senses of the word. As one commentator noted, 'it was a lucrative business for some riders, particularly if you can put up a great sprint now and again, just to make the fellows who want to win understand the necessity of paying you not to'.

Some tried to justify the teaming. They claimed that it was an open, fair technique and that 'the men divided the cash on the track in the presence of officials'. *The Town & Country Journal* pointed out that, in accepting teaming, the men rode clean and free, with no elbowing and no looking around. In that sense, it continued, the sport was 'far ahead of that in America'. One Sydney newspaper commented, 'With all due deference to the champion [Major Taylor], who sets up such high moral standards and apparently thanks God that he is not like other men, and Australian cyclists, cycle racing is as fair here as in any part of the world and fairer than in America from all accounts. For that matter, many of the tricks of the game have been brought here by Americans'. Many possibly, but not all.

Given his acknowledged superior abilities, Major Taylor realised that his arguments for abolishing Australian handicap racing only appeared to be an effort to feather his own nest. He simply had to live with the situation. Fortunately, with his skill he did not suffer unduly—except in The Sydney Thousand. There, in the highest paying cycle race in the world, with first prize alone worth over four years of an average worker's salary, the temptations were too great. When nearly the entire group of Australian riders put their mind to it even the Major did not have a chance.

❖ ❖ ❖

The Sydney Thousand was so named because there was a total of £1,000 prize money: £750 for first place, £100 for second place, and £50 for third place. The remainder was divided among the winners of various qualifying heats. Riders came from all around Australia to take their chances against New Zealanders, Englishmen, Italians, Irishmen, Canadians, and Danes. Major Taylor received £500 simply to appear. A series of cycle races had just been completed in Victoria and the railways put on sets of special carriages to convey some 80 riders and their trainers, machines and retinue back to Sydney. Among Taylor's opponents was the sole other American, Norman Hopper, who had only recently arrived in the country.

The qualifying heats and final race were held at the Sydney Cricket Ground. It was spectacular at night, with the grandstands lit by electric lights and the track by overhanging acetylene gas lamps. Simultaneous with the firing of the starter's gun the grandstand lights were turned off, leaving all attention focused upon the lighted track and riders. In every effort to pack in the patrons the promoters also hired two touring German motorcyclists, Robl and Dickentman, who gave a speed demonstration and paced the cyclists during their warm-up laps. As it was Taylor's farewell appearance in New South Wales, special excursion trains were also scheduled from a number of country towns.

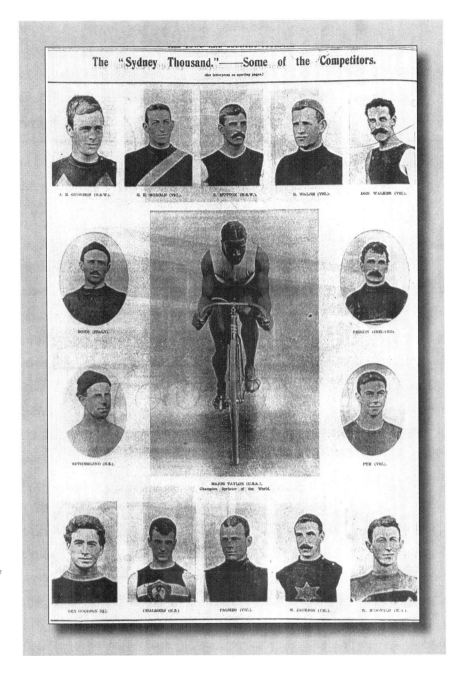

The Town and Country Journal's, 'stars' of the 1903 Sydney Thousand did not include the recently-arrived American, Norman Hopper, who won the race

The qualifying heats for The Sydney Thousand were spread over several nights to ensure that no rider had to put out undue effort in any given evening. One hundred and fifteen cyclists paid entry fees; only 11 would make it to the final. The handicaps of the riders ranged from 5 yards to 240 yards. Taylor alone started from scratch.

In his first qualifying heat Major Taylor was paired off with Don Walker. According to observers Taylor had to ride the hardest portion of the race alone, 'owing to the want of an agreement' among the back markers, and appeared to have 'considerable difficulty' finishing in third position. Taylor, however, said that he had qualified 'handily'.

In the semi-final heat the Major set out with the back markers to catch the front field. Again, Taylor's fellow back markers did not pace 'worth a cent', owing to a misunderstanding or 'something else', and allowed the front bunch to get an uncatchable lead. The horrified officials realised that their biggest drawcard was about to be eliminated from the final of The Sydney Thousand. They immediately declared it 'no race' and ordered all riders off the track.

The failure of the back markers to ride forcefully was seen by one newspaper as 'the most disgraceful bit of sport ever seen in Sydney'. The crowd hooted them. Some fans and sports writers were so incensed that they felt that all of the back markers except the Major should have been permanently banned from cycle racing. But not everyone felt that way. One journalist questioned why the riders should be penalised because of a want of judgment. The officials, however, did not consider it a 'want of judgment'. They saw it as collusion. Taylor said that a number of the riders had 'gotten their heads together' and decided that he would not win unless he entered into an agreement with them. He refused any agreement. They kept their heads together.

The Major's semi-final qualifying heat was re-run the following Monday night. The result was identical. The other back markers appeared to have 'lost interest' in catching the front bunch. Taylor could not reach the leaders and failed to qualify for the final of The

Sydney Thousand. Bill MacDonald, a West Australian, was seen as the principal culprit and was hooted by the crowd throughout the remainder of the evening. The race result was allowed to stand although, as many pointed out, there was as least as much cause, if not more, for ruling it 'no race' than there had been on the previous Saturday. Major Taylor said that he could have bought his way into the final but was 'out here to win races, not buy them'. Don Walker felt that it was 'a heavy indictment of Australian cycling'.

Not everyone felt that it was a clear-cut case of good and evil. *The Arrow*, normally a Taylor supporter, said that it was 'simply bunkum to talk of the "immorality" of combinations of pacing men and to sneer at the "buying" of races'. If Taylor had offered the back men a bit of the prize in anticipation of his success, there would have been nothing in it to hurt 'either his or any other tender conscience. He should have nous [intelligence] enough to fall in with the customs of the country in which he is racing. He, or no other rider, could win it alone, and it is expecting too much of human nature and professional sport to require the rest of the field to generously work their hardest to enable him to win'.

The final of The Sydney Thousand was run according to the traditional Australian team concept of handicap racing. It boiled down to one team headed by Norman Hopper, the American, against another headed by Don Walker. The result was an Australian record. To that extent, handicap team riding had proved its merits in providing an extremely exciting, record-setting race. It also spread the money around. Hopper, the winner, by his own admission paid out £500 of the £750 first prize to his pacing colleagues.

The latter fact starkly highlights the disparity between Taylor's income and that of the other riders that season. The Major received some £4,000 in three months, did not share any, and was about to set off to Europe with at least that much again in his sights.

Newspaper accounts indicated that Don Walker's £808 of winnings was the second highest total that season, behind Taylor, but he also shared some around (how much is not known). If he paid out from a third to a half of it, he would have netted only about 10–15 per cent of the Major's income. Hopper's £750 Sydney Thousand win made him the third highest earner on the circuit that season. His £250 net, however, after paying out other riders, was only six per cent of the Major's season take. From that perspective it is understandable why so many backmarkers became restless about Taylor's refusal to share his winnings with them. He could not have won without their assistance, as several races showed, yet they had nothing to show for it.

The row over The Sydney Thousand scandal had begun to subside as Taylor prepared to leave Australia, but not before some strong words had been uttered. The promoters were accused of 'grafting at the game for gold alone', and the officials taken to task for not giving due consideration to the 'purity' of bicycle racing. It was felt by many that the management of the races did not auger well for the sport's future. As events were to prove, it was an astute assessment. By the time the next season finished Australians could be justified in asking if the concept of 'sport' fitted at all.

PART 2

The Second Australian Tour

"Poisoned Minds"

Christchurch,
New Zealand,
1900

52

4. Down Under Again

At the end of the 1903 Australian tour the Major and his wife sailed to Europe for the third time. When Taylor landed on the Continent the European season was well underway and the local cyclists fit. Taylor attempted to regain form quickly but it was difficult as he spent much of his time on trains dashing from one track to another, losing several races in the process. Once he overcame his initial fitness problems, however, he had a highly successful tour, defeating champions and former champions from Holland, Denmark, France, Italy, and England, among others, as well as American Owen Kimble, one of the Major's bitter rivals who was touring Europe that summer. Sid Jenkins, a Welshman who won numerous National Cyclists' Union's professional championships in England, summed it up for many competitors: 'I have been beaten by the fastest rider in the world today'. The Major returned to America with an estimated £6,000.

In Australia, the success of the Major's European tour was both good news and bad news for Hugh McIntosh's syndicate, which was thinking about bringing him back Down Under. It was good news in that it showed that he was still the force to be reckoned with on the world's cycling tracks and could still draw crowds. The bad news, however, had two aspects. For one thing, the Major wanted more money. That was no obstacle if the spectators kept coming in sufficient numbers. But therein lay the second problem. As one Sydney newspaper put it, there was doubt as to whether large crowds would routinely flock to the tracks again to see the 'Flying Darkie' regularly beat the Australians in honest races.

To resolve the matter, McIntosh's Sydney Summer Nights Amusement Committee sent Tom Scott touring the world 'looking for cycling stars and other novelties'. The Major was reported from England as saying that 'the betting evil Down Under is responsible for much dishonest riding', suggesting he might be less than keen to return. Nonetheless the syndicate made him an offer. It was refused, but not from lack of interest. Taylor simply felt the proposed tour program was too long, involved too many races, and would affect his European tour the following summer. He countered by asking for £2,000 tour money ($700,000 modern day wage equivalent) and no more than three races per week, over three months. This forced the promoters to think hard. For one thing the Melbourne Bicycle Club would not contribute to the Major's tour fund because he would be arriving too late for the Austral Wheel Race in Melbourne, the country's second biggest event. Ultimately McIntosh agreed to Taylor's terms, but only after Tom Scott slid a pair of aces up his sleeve.

❖ ❖ ❖

After the successful season in Europe and a brief rest in their Massachusetts home the Taylors headed back Down Under. They took a train to San Francisco and boarded a ship for New Zealand in November, 1903. Their destination was Christchurch, in the South Island, at that time equal in size to Auckland. It was the site of the New Zealand Wheel Race, the country's foremost event.

The Taylors arrived at Lyttelton, the port town near Christchurch, on Thursday morning, the 10th of December. They were met by representatives of the Christchurch Cycling and Motor Club and George Sutherland, the New Zealand cycling champion. The Major had suffered seasickness for much of the journey and *The Canterbury Times* journalist who met him at the dock noted that 'for such a travelled individual he is the poorest of sailors, and the present trip from America has left him thoroughly tired out'. He went on to describe for his readers the 'greatest celebrity in the cycle racing world … a full-blooded negro, the broad nose and lips, snowy white teeth that fairly glisten in their whiteness, and the blackest of black hair'.

During the train ride from the port to Christchurch the writer tried to elicit various comments from Taylor but initially found it difficult. 'His mono-syllabic answers and unresponsive manner suggested a taciturn demeanour that has not been coupled with his reputation'. However, when the journalist referred to the racism of white riders on American tracks Taylor 'abandoned his reserve … and "found his tongue"'.

The party first dropped Daisy off at Warner's Hotel, over-looking Cathedral Square, where the Taylors would reside during their brief stay. The men then went straight out to visit the Canada

Members of a motor-cycling club outside Warner's Hotel, 1904

Cycle and Motor Company's depot. Taylor inspected his bicycle 'in every detail' and ordered a one and one-eighth inch tyre mounted on the front wheel, and a one inch on the rear.

After the long sea voyage Taylor's fitness was a major concern: 'It has always been a rule of mine not to race until I've been able to get into good form'. He pointed out to the press that 'some people have a notion that a race track is kept aboard ship for me and that as soon as I land at a place I can race right away'. That not being the case he engaged the services of Charles Brown-Parker, a local 'boxing identity', to help with his fitness preparations during the 10 days before his first race. Brown-Parker was an American who had come south about 1900, calling himself 'Kid' Parker. He circulated throughout Australia and New Zealand, developing a contentious reputation. He worked on the Rickard Vaudeville circuit and in the year prior to Taylor's arrival was billed as giving a 'magnificent display of ball punching'. It was the only thing he was fit for, *The Truth*, in Melbourne, later wrote, as his pu-

Charles Brown-Parker gilistic talents 'existed only in

his imagination'. His talents were sufficient, however, to enable him to severely beat a *Truth* editor, in his office, some years later.

The meet took place over two days at the Lancaster Park track. The Kiwis had high expectations. The first afternoon, Wednesday, December 16, saw 8,000 spectators turn out, the largest crowd ever to attend a cycle race in Christchurch. However, the attendance was not due solely to Taylor's appearance—it was bolstered by the five mile New Zealand Motor-Cycle Wheel Race also on the card that afternoon.

The two-mile New Zealand Wheel Race was the feature and George Sutherland was given a 40-yard handicap over Taylor, who started from scratch. The Major complained, noting that he had not been on a bicycle for over two months prior to his arrival. Nonetheless the handicapper 'maintained his right' to handicap Taylor based on his best performance. After the race began Taylor finally managed to catch Sutherland, but the latter had caught up with another backmarker who was pacing him. Another rider between Taylor and the Sutherland pair engaged in some 'irregular' riding, with the result that Taylor realised he could not catch Sutherland and dropped out of the race. The Major, generous with his praise, refused to offer any excuses. 'I wish to say nothing to detract from Mr Sutherland's victory. I take off my hat to him and congratulate him on winning a fair, hard-run race. It was his day and he deserves all the credit'.

Taylor did not ride again that afternoon. As a result there were many in the crowd 'who had never been to a bicycle meeting before and are very unlikely to go again'. Expecting to see more of Taylor, many felt that they had been 'taken in'. Consequently, only 3,500 people showed up for that night's session, when the Major contested a mile race. He was again handicapped severely and finished fourth.

On Saturday afternoon, the 19th, Taylor competed in another mile race before just 3,000 onlookers. He won his heat but in the

George Sutherland

final 'got into rather a bad position' among other riders and lost to Sutherland. That island nation had just witnessed the poorest overall performance in the Major's entire career. Before leaving the country he asked reporters to express to their readers his regret at not having been able to do himself justice in New Zealand.

Taylor's failures could not be put down simply to a lack of fitness, though. Before dropping out of the race on that first Wednesday afternoon, he had pedalled an unaided lap around the large oval in 43 seconds, four seconds faster than the previous track record. He was clearly a competitive rider. However, it was reported that the 'irregular' riding that had caused him to drop out resulted from other competitors having made arrangements between themselves with the specific aim of defeating Taylor. Afterward race officials agreed that Taylor had not received fair play but took no action. Combined with the huge handicaps, the Major was never in contention.

After Daisy and the Major departed, *The Canterbury Times'* cycling writer assessed the unsatisfactory situation he had witnessed in New Zealand, and added: 'It will be surprising to me if Major Taylor has not more troubles ahead when he reaches Australia. Fresh from the tossing about of another sea trip, he will be called to straightaway race the Americans, MacFarland and Lawson'.

*Stands at the Coolgardie cycle
track, Western Australia, 1896*

5. MacFarland and Lawson

Floyd MacFarland and Iver Lawson were the two aces up the sleeve of the Sydney Summer Nights Amusement Committee. They were among the very best cyclists in the world. Of particular importance, from the syndicate's perspective, was the pair's intense desire to defeat Major Taylor and their proven ability to do so. MacFarland and Lawson, driven by both professional cycling ambition and racial antipathy, had clashed with Taylor on many occasions, both on and off track. There was no love lost.

The three proved explosive—personally, professionally and promotionally. Their contests were always tense and exciting, often spectacular, and resulted in several new Australian and world records. They drew huge crowds to the tracks yet frequently left those crowds frustrated and angry. Nonetheless the patrons came back for more and that was what cycle race promotion was all about.

Floyd MacFarland, from San Jose, California, was one of America's great cycling talents, and a powerful influence on the sport for 25 years. At 6 feet 4 inches tall he was a striking figure and attracted large crowds with his personality and riding talent. MacFarland held numerous world records during his career and by the time he came to Australia had won hundreds of events in the United States and abroad. Frank Kramer, American champion, considered Floyd the best all around biker in the world: 'MacFarland was so far superior to every other rider, it was not even close. He would win a sprint race one day, a pursuit and pace race the next, a six-day race and then ask the boys if they knew of any other games'.

MacFarland never won the American championship but came close several times, finishing second and third. However, as one New York journalist put it, on more than one occasion Floyd determined who *would* wear the crown, both by defeating riders himself, and managing others. He was particularly good at managing. Kramer won the American championship in 1901 under MacFarland's personal supervision. But Floyd's interests were not altruistic. As Major Taylor commented, 'MacFarland was a good manager—for MacFarland'. Floyd made more money through overseeing Kramer's championship season than he did from his own winnings on the track that year.

In 1900, MacFarland proposed teaming up with Taylor as co-rider and manager. They would start by combining in the Madison Square Garden six-day race. On the strength of that presumed victory and their joint reputations they could virtually dictate tour terms to the Europeans the next season. 'By no stretch of the imagination could he have been termed friendly to me' Taylor said. However, Floyd, the hard-headed businessman, was willing to put animosities aside. He saw gold in Europe.

On the Continent the track owners paid for trainers and masseurs (which the riders had to personally finance in America), the promoters offered up to £400 per race for first prize, and training and travel expenses would be covered by the cycle manufacturers with whom the riders were under contract. MacFarland went so far as to propose an itinerary for the 1901 season. Taylor turned him down. The momentary armistice between them was short lived and MacFarland was 'peeved'. The Major paid the price from that time on.

Floyd MacFarland was intelligent, shrewd, well educated and a natural judge of men. He made effective use of his dominant personality and 'determined countenance'. Curly Grivell, an Australian cyclist, spoke of MacFarland's 'convincing manner of arguing; his word was law. He was a natural born leader, an effective demonstrator of plans and schemes, and whatever he said went with the rank and file of the riders; they would follow him through thick and thin'. However, he led them into some murky waters and not everyone liked what they saw. One Australian rider saw in Floyd an 'absolute bully, who was aggressive and bad-mouthed in every way. He was a first-class cyclist and a second-class citizen'.

The dark side to MacFarland's character was his systematic, obsessive campaign against Major Taylor. Floyd directed substantial energies toward, and appeared to derive much motivation from, attempts to stymie the Major's career. Taylor said bluntly that MacFarland was 'the ringleader of the gang of riders who had sworn among themselves to bring about my dethronement'. Near the end of his life Taylor acknowledged that he had been taught that 'one should "speak naught but good of the dead"', but nonetheless he would always remember the late Floyd MacFarland as 'the instigator and leading perpetrator of practically all the underhanded scheming' that brought about his failure to win any more American championship laurels after 1900.

Floyd MacFarland

MacFarland's efforts weren't confined to the track. He conducted an all-round campaign of psychological and physical intimidation of Taylor. The Major wrote that it became so extreme that on one occasion he used a piece of two-by-four timber to defend himself

Iver Lawson

and his trainer from a physical attack by MacFarland, Lawson and Kramer until the police arrived. Understandably, Taylor was bitter.

Iver Lawson was an extremely swift, talented cyclist. Born Yver Larsson, in Norrkopping, Sweden, where he rode for the local cycling club, he migrated to America with his family and changed his name. After a period of riding with the Swedish-American cycling club in Chicago he ended up in Salt Lake City. In 1898, the year in which Major Taylor won his first American championship, the 19-year-old Lawson finished thirteenth—but Iver was on his way up. He went to Australia for the 1900-1901 season and scored numerous victories before his tour was cut short by injuries in Adelaide. He returned home and finished third in the US championships.

In 1902, MacFarland, who knew a good thing when he saw it, took Lawson under his wing. As Iver commented to an Australian scribe two years later, Floyd 'knows exactly how to train a man, and he has taught me all I know. When I started with him I thought I knew a good deal, but soon found out that I knew nothing'. MacFarland had taught him well—and was not yet finished. The 164 pound, 5 foot 11 inch 'Speedy Swede' from Salt Lake City, Utah, was using Australia as a lucrative training ground for bigger and better things. In a few months MacFarland's protégé was to win the world's championship at the Crystal Palace in London.

MacFarland and Lawson arrived in Australia several weeks before Taylor and quickly made their mark on the national cycling circuit. They willingly gave the local riders valuable tips about training, something they had reduced to a fine art. On the track MacFarland and Lawson proved so fast that as a team they were generally able to outpace any Australian opponents or combination of them. It appeared that the only way to defeat the pair was to handicap them right out of the race. They complained that this in fact happened on a number of occasions. But the local riders could be forgiven for asking when. As *The Australian Cyclist* pointed out, by February, 1904 Iver Lawson alone had won an astounding 18 firsts, 5 seconds and 4 thirds around the country. *The Sydney Sportsman*'s advice to bettors was to 'put your spare bob on the Yankee every time'. They were so successful that one writer, in a letter-to-the-editor, complained that the pair's monotonous wins would kill the interest in cycling. 'At least', he wrote, 'Taylor sometimes lost'.

Cycle racing in Coolgardie, on the Western Australian goldfields, 1896

Start of the Westral Wheel, Coolgardie, 1896

Notwithstanding their dominance, the American duo proved immensely popular with other cyclists, the promoters, and the crowds. Australians appreciate and respect sporting talent and MacFarland and Lawson certainly had that in abundance. Everywhere they went people paid to see it.

However, the pair quickly demonstrated a knack for leaving controversy in their wake. At the Westral Wheel race in Western Australia, the third richest in the country, officials banned Lawson from the final for having 'pulled up' in a qualifying heat and allowing another rider to finish ahead of him. It was suspected that Lawson had deliberately thrown the race because he or MacFarland had bet heavily on the competitor. Iver's banishment from the final was no worry for the high-powered American pair, however. MacFarland simply mounted his machine and pedalled away with the £400 first prize.

But the most critical—and continuing—controversy Down Under swirled about the arrangements that MacFarland routinely made to attempt to defeat Major Taylor. Given his force of character and ability to dominate other riders, his superb cycling skills, his management of a highly gifted protégé, and his inclination to *make* arrangements, MacFarland found a fruitful field for exploitation. And exploit he did, to the Major's great detriment.

No one was in a better position to appreciate the situation than Hugh McIntosh. Later in life, reflecting upon his career and promotion of many boxing matches in Australia and abroad, he said that 'there was never anything crooked about one'. As to cycling, however, 'my experiences were less happy'; it was one of 'the dirtiest sports in Australia'.

The Bulletin
*mastheads from
1902 (above) and
1910.*

6. A Chill in the Air

Major Taylor came ashore in Sydney on Wednesday, December 23, 1903, with his 'light buoyant step and graceful carriage'. *The Daily Telegraph* moved articles about him from the sports pages to the news pages. At his request the number 13 had been reserved for his use. Mr and Mrs E.B. Lumley of Surrey Hills expressed their friendliness to 'worthy strangers in a strange land' by throwing an all night bash for the 'Yankee fliers'—though there was no indication the Taylors attended. The 1904 cycling season was underway.

During January Sydney would host four International Test races. Interspersed between them, and continuing on into February and March, the riders would be journeying between Melbourne, Adelaide and Sydney on a seemingly endless cycling merry-go-round. They would be riding in the Commonwealth Stakes, the Furracabad Handicap, the McCullagh Plate, the Druids' Gala ... the list went on and on, crowned with The Sydney Thousand. It was a cycling feast, the banquet table was heaped with prize money, and the Americans had come to dine.

In exchange for the £2,000 tour fee all of the Major's appearances were controlled by McIntosh's Sydney Summer Nights Amusement Committee. As to MacFarland and Lawson, both Major Taylor and contemporary newspaper reports indicated that the white duo's only income throughout the tour was from local appearance fees and their success on the track.

In MacFarland's case, however, 'success on the track' could mean many things. Almost before he lost his sea legs Taylor discovered a formidable combination of riders arrayed against him and found himself confronted with a degree of jealousy, bitterness and racial hatred unlike anything he had experienced during the previous season. It resulted directly from Floyd MacFarland's efforts and centred about a retinue of white American riders. In addition to MacFarland and Lawson, Orlando Stevens, highly antagonistic towards Taylor, and Hardy Downing had also come to Australia. According to the Major, MacFarland had proposed to them that they combine against Taylor during the tour, pool their winnings, and split them evenly at the end.

But the Americans did not act alone and in fact could not. Given the various heats involved in reaching the finals of the major races and the talents of many of the Australians, Floyd's proposal would require them to be included in the arrangements. Thus during his first weeks in Australia MacFarland, the 'king-pin of the schemers', stirred the local riders. There were many ready listeners among them.

Floyd emphasised the obvious. Major Taylor was already well paid for his Australian tour and would receive yet additional local appearance fees, aside from any prize money and bonuses. The others would ultimately end up doing the 'donkey work' only to watch the shrewd tactician and physically superior Taylor sprint around them at the finish. There would be no sharing of winnings. The implications were not lost on the Australians. They had seen that very thing happen time and again in early 1903. Worse, they now had to contend with MacFarland and Lawson as well. The local riders sensed the elemental truth in that old adage, 'if you can't lick them ...'.

There is an important economic factor that played a role in the Australian riders' change of attitude. Australia (with the exception of Western Australia) was still not fully recovered from the deep depression of the 1890s. Economic historians indicate that it was every bit as serious as the 1930s depression (some suggest even more so) and lasted as long. The young riders had thus grown up in a period of scarce jobs, low pay and general hardship. In that context Major Taylor's take of some £4,000 in 1903 could have been seen as unjustifiable, if not obscene. And Taylor was back again with a bigger tour fee in hand. Any offers by MacFarland and Lawson to share winnings in exchange for 'arrangements' would have looked very attractive to the Australians. The two experienced, world-class riders were their only real hope of keeping Taylor from walking away yet again with the bulk of the season's prize money.

Notwithstanding the economics of the situation the Major found it 'a strange revelation' at how fast MacFarland's 'propaganda' took hold among the Australian riders, in particular with Don Walker. On the first tour Taylor found him a gentleman, a keen rival, and fair, not 'an unpleasant word having passed between us'. In 1904 there was a 'complete turnabout'. Although Walker was never outspoken towards him Taylor sensed that Don's mind had been 'poisoned'.

The Major felt that MacFarland's 'most cowardly weapon' was his use of racism. The basis was quite simple as far as the Sydney *Worker* was concerned: 'Lawson and MacFarland hate Taylor, whom they regard as most Americans do [black Americans]'. In the United States at that time racism was probably at its most virulent. With the abolition of slavery four decades earlier the American south, in particular, had to come to grips with a radical new social order. By 1900 a series of 'Jim Crow' laws and extralegal actions had been instituted establishing segregated drinking facilities, restaurants, toilets, hotels, residential areas and transport facilities—in effect delineating a separate society. This social milieu, albeit less blatantly, existed in many parts of the northern United States as well. In essence, while much of white America was erecting powerful racial barriers Major Taylor was breaching some of them. His skill, earnings, demand and celebrity status utterly galled many white racist Americans, and none more so than Floyd MacFarland.

In Australia Floyd made no secret of his hatred of Taylor or of the fact that he would stop at nothing to beat him, while Iver Lawson made his own feelings about Taylor clear in an interview given during the season: 'We never speak, and we pass in the street without noticing one another'. As one newspaper confirmed, 'race prejudice and professional jealousy work together'. The jealousies were further inflamed by the fact that the 'Black Cyclone' had his own separate tent at the big cycle meets while the other riders had to share facilities. That did not sit well in some circles.

Hints of racism in the coming season surfaced shortly before Lawson and MacFarland arrived. The Melbourne *Argus* commented that 'Although the colour line is not drawn in Australia as it is in the "land of the free", the cyclists generally will be better pleased to see Lawson or MacFarland carrying off the rich prizes than they would to see Taylor succeed. As long as they "play the game", the visitors can be assured of good treatment'. Some journalists tried to play down racial motives, suggesting that the antipathy to Major Taylor was caused simply because he would not team and pay his colleagues a dividend for pacing. Yet, a few weeks later the same paper commented that 'Australian cyclists seem to draw the colour line ... 9/10 of the Aussie riders, for diverse reasons—cash, colour and otherwise—have been out of sympathy with him, and the antagonism has grown with each meeting'. The Major's widely publicised piety provided another hook upon which to hang cynical grievances. One correspondent's comment about his £2,000 tour fee was that 'the Pious Taylor always asserts that the Lord will provide for him, but he does not leave anything to chance'.

There is little evidence that the Australian race-going public felt the same. It seems that Major Taylor was exempted from the underlying racism that existed in the country. He was a visitor, a world class talent, and a legend. The Australians respected Taylor and no newspaper report, nor Taylor himself, ever suggested that they taunted him. In fact, as it became obvious during the tour that the Major was battling severe odds he gained increasing sympathy from the Australian crowds. Whatever racial-financial basis the riders had for colluding against Taylor, the Major was not threatening the fans' livelihood or professional ego. They simply wanted to see the world's best cyclist in action—in fair races. It was a strange turn of events. In a country self-avowedly noted for cutting down 'tall poppies', the tallest cycling poppy of them all—Major Taylor—suddenly found himself the underdog. As they say Down Under, 'you wouldn't credit it'.

One view of the public reaction to Major Taylor was given by *The Sunday Times* newspaper, via a fictional conversation with the Australian Prime Minister, Alfred Deakin. To appreciate it, it is necessary to understand how the Australian government kept out undesirables. A display in the Immigration Museum, housed in the Old Customs House, in Melbourne, explains it:

> From 1901 customs officers were given the power to exclude all non-Europeans. This became the cornerstone of the so-called White Australia Policy. In the face of considerable international criticism, officials looked for a way to exclude people without making it seem due to race. The answer was the notorious Dictation Test. Immigrants could be required to pass a language test in any European language. If they failed, they were refused entry.

In practice Customs Officers would read a passage to undesirables, who had to write down what was said and sign it. One Customs Officer said that they even made up their own tests, such as 'The harassed pedlar met the embarrassed cobbler in the cemetery gauging the symmetry of a lady's ankle in unparalleled ecstasy.' When undesired intending migrants failed to transcribe the dictations accurately they were refused entry. The Dictation Test could also be used to exclude undesirable white Europeans. One political activist who spoke several European languages eventually failed only when he was tested in Gaelic.

> 'Mr. Deakin? We regret to be the bearer of an unpleasant message, Sir, but there is an immigrant at large who was not given the Greek test.'
> 'Perhaps he was of Greek nationality.'
> 'No. This unprohibited prohibited alien is an American citizen and came out here under contract. He is a coloured alien, uniting in his own person all the dire things that the Act was intended to save this new country from. May we further inform you that this coloured contract-alien expects to escape with a creditable haul of some thousands of pounds?'
> 'Impossible! Is he a mental or manual worker?'
> 'Neither, he is a pedal worker—Major Taylor!'
> 'Ah. You know quite well that the Act was made both rigid and elastic. It has to be stretched sometimes.'

The Major considered it 'amusing'.

By the end of the 1902 season in North America Major Taylor had apparently made the decision to never again race in the United States. The continuing difficulty of finding food and accommodation while travelling, the physical threats, and the venomous racism he encountered over the years had taken their toll. When combined with the absolute determination of MacFarland and other riders to prevent him from winning another American sprint championship the Major could read the writing on the wall. The strain and money to be found there were simply not worth it. Indeed, the situation had become intolerable.

The offer to come to Australia in late 1902 proved to be a timely and welcome relief. The joy of the first Australian tour and subsequent success in Europe were in striking contrast to circumstances in his home country. The financial, professional and personal satisfactions of the two 1903 overseas tours led him to arrange a return trip to Australia in their 1903–1904 summer and another European tour in the northern summer of 1904. He was in a position to earn a comfortable living without ever again having to face the evils of the American racing circuit.

Teaming and racism were not new to the Major, of course. They were just part and parcel of a frequently witnessed scenario. While the early 1904 performance was in a different country, with a different supporting cast, and different crowds, it had the same leading characters and the same tedious plot. In contrast to previous experiences, however, the forthcoming Australian enactment, with MacFarland and Lawson on the stage, would turn out to be a devastating tragedy for Taylor. They visited upon him a terrible affliction of hard-fought, rigged races at the end of which Taylor would effectively collapse emotionally and physically. He earned every shilling that season.

*Theodore Robl,
R. McCullagh
(Secretary of the
Melbourne Bicycle
Club and patron of
the McCullagh Plate
race) and Taylor,
at the Melbourne
Exhibition Ground
track*

7. Rough Tactics

With less than a fortnight to train and recover from his sea journey, Major Taylor launched himself into the competition on January 1, 1904. The four International Test races spaced throughout the month comprised an elite series and only 20 riders were selected. The first three races were over a half mile, four miles, and five miles, respectively. The finishers were awarded one point for first, two for second, and so on. Those with the lowest number of points would compete in the final one mile Test. The winner of that race would be crowned series champion and receive all the prize money.

The crowd that packed the ground on the opening night was immense and tense with excitement, for the term 'Test' has a particular significance in Commonwealth countries. Circa 1884 the term 'test matches' was first applied to a series of intensely competitive cricket encounters between Australia and England. As Australian historian Ken Inglis noted, the phrase came to suggest 'more than mere play', It was, in effect, an 'ordeal, a proving, a trial', That was indeed the case with the International Test cycling races. The very first meet set the pattern for the season: no quarter given or asked; hard riding and dangerous tactics; stunning results; harried officials; and spectacular, bitterly vindictive bicycle racing.

Taylor, Lawson, MacFarland and Don Walker each won their respective half-mile heats, and lined up for the final race. They were paced halfway by Boidi, a visiting Italian. From the start the race was very fast. When Boidi pulled out, Taylor was in front. Immediately MacFarland and Lawson shot past him on the outside. As MacFarland

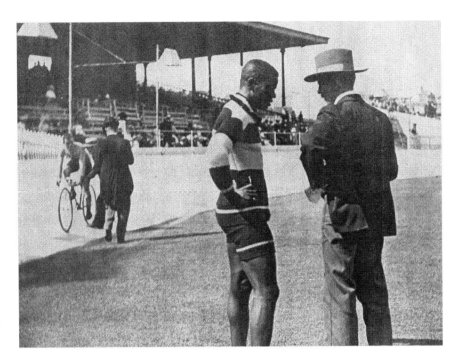

Taylor at the Sydney Cricket Ground

pulled into the lead he cut sharply back in, forcing Taylor on to the grass. When the Major pulled back on the track Lawson was on his outside, trapping him in a pocket. Knowing that it was impossible to beat the pair from that position, Taylor suddenly dropped back and pulled around to the outside of Lawson. But it was too late. By then MacFarland had crossed the line, with Lawson behind him, Taylor third and Walker fourth.

The crowds booed MacFarland while the stewards conferred with the referee. They concluded that not only had Taylor been un-fairly interfered with by Lawson and MacFarland but that the three of them, in their struggle, had prevented Walker from getting a fair ride. They declared it a 'no race'. The crowd cheered; they were satis-fied with the decision and would get more for their money that night than they had bargained on.

When the four were called back for the re-ride, Lawson and MacFarland, venting their spite and anger, refused to race. It was their privilege but it wasn't popular with the crowd or officials and there was renewed booing. Don Walker, the Australian champion, was now left to face Major Taylor alone. The starter sent them on their way behind another pacer; when he dropped off Taylor leapt forward. However, Walker stayed right with him and around the track they sprinted, side by side. The cheers were deafening as the two men dashed for the tape and threw themselves across the line together. The excitement remained at a fever pitch as the judges met. They finally announced their decision—a dead heat, the points to be divided equally between Taylor and Walker. The crowd roared their approval. Australia's own champion had matched the Major man for man.

Three days later MacFarland was suspended for a month for forcing Taylor on to the grass. The decision was widely applauded, but not universally. MacFarland had his supporters. One correspondent to *The Sydney Morning Herald* felt that Floyd had been unfairly treated. His only crime was to show that Taylor, 'the £2,000 big gun', had finally 'met his Waterloo'. The writer suggested that MacFarland would remove much of the glamour that had hung around Taylor 'like a halo'.

Floyd appealed the suspension. A week later the Council of the League of Wheelmen met and reconsidered the matter. They decided that he was rightly disqualified but, since he had missed two races in the interim, he would be reinstated if he paid a £25 fine. It was said to be a good 'warning' to other riders. Rumour had it, however, that the syndicate was 'aghast' at the loss of one of its two big drawcards at the start of the season and had put considerable pressure on the Council to modify the punishment. Given that Hugh McIntosh, the syndicate leader, was Secretary of the League and on the Council, and Paddy O'Brien, another syndicate member, was a League official, the Sydney Summer Nights Amusement Committee was certainly in a position to influence matters.

Several days later the four-mile race was held. The promoters had shrewdly offered prize money for the leader of each lap and the race was extremely fast. It was an all-American contest from the start. At the bell lap, the four white Americans shot around Taylor. The Major could not work his way through the combination and finished half a length behind Lawson. In the five-mile race later that month it came down to the final lap between MacFarland, Taylor and Lawson. Taylor and Lawson bumped but no one complained; Lawson won that race in world record time and everyone gave credit where it was due. The crowds were getting their money's worth.

The extensive teaming against Taylor was becoming obvious and many did not like it. Some tried blaming it all on the Americans. *The Town & Country Journal*, in suggesting that teaming was introduced by the Yanks only a few months before, was conveniently forgetting its own cycling scandals.

The grand finale of the International Test series was held at the end of January at the Sydney Cricket Ground. The crowd of 30,000 was 'seized with the vastness and effect' when the grandstand lights were turned off, leaving the track highlighted. It was a fitting setting for the cycling spectacle. The fourth and final Test, over one mile, included Bill MacDonald, from Western Australia, Hardy Downing, Taylor and Lawson. The most astonishing aspect was that Taylor had yet to score a Test victory. He had managed only a dead heat with Walker, and two seconds behind Lawson.

The race began with George Farley and Ben Goodson, the two pacers, changing position every half lap. They dropped out at the bell. The crowd arose in one mass, screaming, as Taylor and Lawson sprinted out of the last turn into the straight. Taylor, with his spectacular jump, outsprinted Lawson to the finish line. The shouting could be heard miles away. Major Taylor had walked away with the lion's share of the Test series prize money by winning only a single race out of the four, but it was the 'most popular win ever known in Sydney, where the darky's gallant struggles against unfair tactics and inferior conditions have made him many friends'.

The see-saw battles continued into February. In Melbourne, at the Australian Natives' Association's Gold Stakes, Taylor and Mac-Farland met in a one-mile race. When Taylor and MacFarland turned into the final stretch Floyd was in the lead 'going for all he knew'. It appeared he could not be beaten. At that point 'Taylor removed one hand from his handlebars, wiped his mouth, put his hand back and streaked right past MacFarland'. It was the famous Major Taylor jump and it 'set the big crowd half wild'. In yet another mile event MacFarland and Taylor again found themselves alone, battling for honours, coming out of the last turn. Instead of the expected Taylor jump, however, MacFarland pulled away to a two-length victory.

In the grand final of the National Fete, a five-mile event, Lawson, MacFarland, Orlando Stevens and Taylor paced one another for most of the journey. At the end of the third mile Stevens ran right down on to Taylor. It looked deliberate. A mile further Stevens was suddenly run up against the fence by a 'wobbling' Taylor. That

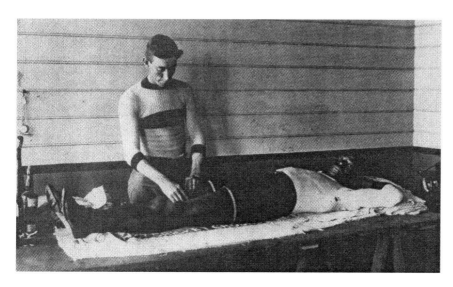

Sid Melville massaging Taylor

looked deliberate too, but the stewards took no action. As one reporter dryly observed, 'they were now even'. An angry Taylor outsprinted everyone over the line.

Things got nastier. In the Melbourne Commonwealth Stakes an Australian rider, Richard Cameron, bored in on the Major. After 'expostulating with him' Taylor shoved him away. When the riders entered the last lap Cameron collided with Taylor, who fell hard opposite the judges. He suffered a deep cut on the arm but was otherwise not badly injured. The Major got up and the spectators cheered him loudly, then booed Cameron. The stewards later disqualified Cameron for a year for elbowing and kneeing Taylor earlier in the race. With respect to the fall itself the stewards felt that the Major was responsible by trying to force himself into an opening that was not there. It would not be the last time that Taylor was accused of that.

The teaming was taking its toll on Taylor. In a mile race a combination nursed Lawson to the final lap and he beat the Major by a wheel. In a ten-mile event that same night the white Americans' combination was 'as plain as a pike staff, even to the palest-faced layman. It was a blood-thirsty race', and Lawson won by two lengths. In a later three-mile event Lawson was again paced to a decisive victory by his team-mates. One journalist commented, 'I hold no brief for Major Taylor, but no man in the world can have a chance against Iver Lawson when he has MacFarland working in his interests'.

As *The Australian Cyclist* observed, Taylor had to rely upon sporadic and disorganised pacing that he might be able to pick up from some Australians. Without systematic help he was going to have a very difficult time ever beating the white American group. The Sydney *Worker* reported that several riders had said that they would not ride in Taylor's circumstances for a fortune. Only his phenomenal cleverness had saved him from severe accidents. Another journalist felt that 'the roguery of cycling—its pocketing, teaming and unfairness—is killing it fast'.

But there was more than roguery to Taylor's defeats and his difficulties could not be attributed solely to combinations. He was not dominating the 1904 season because he was in very fast company. Lawson, in particular, was on a hot streak, setting two five-mile world records in days. In such circumstances every race ridden by the Major was bound to be difficult. The riding was intense, highly competitive and any momentary bump or hesitation could cost a victory. In the heat of the moment with the riders bunched tightly, and Taylor in particular noted for his jerky style and efforts to force himself underneath, it was not surprising that there were some dubious riding incidents—on the part of the Major as well as others.

Thus matters stood. There was simply no predicting what would happen. Lawson, Taylor or MacFarland would seemingly beat one or the other decisively, then be beaten in turn. The combinations the white Americans developed were not invincible, and the Major could give as well as take. When it came to pushing and shoving he was notably aggressive in forcing his way through a pack. MacFarland and Lawson had made it clear they were going to beat Taylor at all costs, but it was equally clear that the Major was not about to be intimidated. As proof, in Sydney he took out several of MacFarland's spokes in a clash on the track. The races may not have been 'fights to the death' but they were very, very dangerous and not for the faint-hearted.

It was inevitable that there be a showdown in Australia between Major Taylor, Floyd MacFarland and Iver Lawson. The white American riders were acknowledged cycling phenomenons in their own right, regardless of the incessant complaints about unfair combinations against Taylor. What everyone really wanted to find out was who was best, man-to-man. They got their chance in February, 1904. By that time the promoters, sensing the mood and smelling more money, and apparently in an ad hoc move outside the originally scheduled tour, made appropriate arrangements.

Swanston Street, Melbourne

8. Melbourne: The Battle of the Champions

The great 'Battle of the Champions' took place in the genteel city of Melbourne, Victoria, with a population of half a million and the temporary capital of the recently formed country. It was long the bicycling capital of Australia. It produced more cycle journals and manufactured more machines than any other city in the country. The Melbourne to Warrnambool Road Race was started in 1895 and is now the second oldest in the world. The Austral Wheel Race, initiated in 1887, is the oldest existing bicycle track race in the world. The cycling extravaganza befitted the city's history and stature.

Given the MacFarland–Lawson manager–rider relationship and the pair's unequivocal hatred of Taylor, the promoters abandoned any plans for a three-way showdown. Instead they opted for three separate man-on-man meets. Besides, if there was money to be made in a great meet there should be thrice as much to be made in three great meets.

The opening races were between Major Taylor and Iver Lawson on Monday night, February 8th. The chosen venue was the Melbourne Exhibition Ground. The track was short, five laps to the mile, and the facility noted for its intense crowd-rider interaction. The format was simple. The pair would meet in three consecutive heats and the first to win two would be the winner and receive the £100 prize money. There was nothing for second place.

On the night 20,000 people turned out despite the fact that a weather front had left the summer evening extremely cold. The crowd, heavily wrapped in overcoats, grew increasingly excited in anticipation. They were finally going to see the two great riders in a 'straight out go', with no other riders, no 'influences', and no 'nursing' of Lawson.

As the starting time drew near for the first race, a half mile, Bill Lewis motored out on the track in his Massey Harris pacing machine. Soon Major Taylor followed and the crowd erupted in cheers as he settled in behind and pedalled a couple of miles to warm up.

The Austral Wheel Race, Melbourne Cricket Ground, 1903

When the time arrived for the start of the race Lawson had not yet appeared. As Taylor rolled up to the starting line, alone, the journalists at the press table looked at one another questioningly, the crowd murmured, and then the stadium went quiet. Where was Lawson? Suddenly a roar erupted as Iver pedalled on to the track. He rode directly to the starting line, pulled up alongside Major Taylor, looked across at the official, and nodded for the race to begin.

The 'Pit' crowd at the Austral Cycling Carnival, Melbourne Cricket Ground

The starter's gun sent them off. The first lap was ridden slowly, both riders staying in the middle of the track. It was obviously going to be a race of great finesse and at that the Major was a master. He forced Lawson into the lead. On the second lap Lawson slowly rode up toward the fence. He was trying to force Taylor into the lead on the inside. Taylor, however, simply remained behind him, watching. Lawson stayed close to the outer railing, up on the bank, eyeing Taylor, preparing for a swift descent. Iver then let his attention lapse momentarily and in an astounding burst the Major leapt past him high on the outside and shot down the bank. Lawson's reaction was too

late. 'In a twinkling of an eye' Taylor had put several lengths between them. The Major crossed the finish line an astonishing six lengths ahead, to the crowd's yells, as 'hats, handkerchiefs, programmes or whatever came handy, were waved in the air'.

After a brief rest the second heat was begun. It was over one mile and was to be paced for four laps by Burton and Walker. When the riders lined up for the start the tension was palpable. The starter fired his pistol and the pacers set off with Taylor close behind. Lawson was very slow to get away and within moments the referee called them back for a re-start.

Iver Lawson

The second time the four led away smoothly in single file. Burton led for three laps then retired and Walker took over for the fourth. The pace had been steady but not overly fast. At the bell lap, when Walker dropped out, Taylor and Lawson slowed markedly. The real race then began. Taylor rapidly manoeuvred Lawson to the front. It was clear that he was the superior tactician. Lawson hugged the railing high on the banking, determined not to be jumped as before. Suddenly, as in the previous race, and at the same spot, the Major made a 'superhuman bound' down the banking, this time on the inside, in full sprint. Lawson was ready, however, and set off after him. Shouts rent the air: 'Had Gabriel sounded his trumpet, they would not have heard'. Major Taylor, 'like a bolt from the blue' had jumped to a several length lead, but as they headed into the straight toward the finish line he was visibly labouring. Lawson put on a phenomenal burst. He was clearly travelling faster than the Major at the finish but Taylor swept across the line two yards ahead.

The crowd was 'delirious'. The soon-to-be world sprinting champion had been defeated in two successive races, jumped first on the outside, and then on the inside, and both times outsprinted to the finish. It had been a true battle of champions—'white, black, yellow or red, never mattered a snuff'—and the issue of who was best had been decided beyond a shadow of a doubt.

Attention could now turn to the upcoming Taylor-MacFarland match. Floyd was much more experienced than Lawson and had personally defeated and coached others to the defeat of Taylor. If the Major was the acknowledged match race champion of the world, MacFarland could still write a respectable textbook of his own. That evening he would give a forceful public reading from it.

EXHIBITION OVAL.

TO-NIGHT   TO-NIGHT

MAJOR TAYLOR V. FLOYD MACFARLAND
Three Mile Heats.
No Dead March Possible. Solid Pace from Begin-
ning to End.

£225   PURSES   £225.
————

The questions of paramount importance at pre-
sent prevailing in the Sporting World are:
"WILL THE BRILLIANT 'MAJOR' SUCCEED IN
OUTGENERALING HIS MIGHTY OPPONENT?"
Or
"WILL THE HUMAN MOTOR'S TRULY PHENO-
MENAL STAMINA WEAR THE 'MAJOR'
DOWN?"

Come and read the answer for yourselves; for
no word-painting will, or can, convey to you any
idea of the exciting interest attached to the grand
struggle that is certain to eventuate at this meeting of
THE WORLD'S CYCLING GIANTS

NOTE:–In consequence of the crush at the recent
Taylor-Lawson match, and in order to prevent a
similar experience at this match, the promoters
have enlarged and perfected the admission space
to such an extent that all inconvenience will be
totally avoided.

Gates open 6.30. First race, 8.

First Heat of Match, 8.50.
ADMISSION, 1/; Stand, 1/ extra.

NEXT WEDNESDAY EVENING,
TAYLOR V. LAWSON,
ONE, TWO, THREE MILES, SOLIDLY PACED

THOS. M. ROBERTSON, Secretary

The Argus, *13th
February, 1904*

9. Taylor Vs. MacFarland

Taylor and MacFarland met on Saturday night, February 13th. Talk of strategies flowed wildly among cycling aficionados during the week. The newspaper advertisement for the race posed the essential question: 'Will the brilliant Major succeed in out-generalling his mighty opponent?' or, 'Will the human motor's truly phenomenal stamina wear the Major down?' It emphasised that 'no word-painting will, or can, convey to you any idea of the exciting interest attached to the grand struggle that is certain to eventuate at this meeting'.

The promoters added extra turnstiles and enlarged the admission area to ease the entry for 20,000 spectators into the compact—and tightly packed—facility. The majority, seeking the best vantage points, were queued up by the time the gates opened at 6.30. They handed over their shilling for admission while thousands paid an additional shilling to get into the grandstand. The summer evening was delightful.

There were a number of preliminary supporting races, heats and finals. When Taylor and MacFarland finally came on the track for the challenge match the crowd erupted in cheers. There they were, the renowned black sprinter and Floyd the warhorse, a 'human motor', a gritty man 'who could race for a mile and still have something in reserve for the finishing burst'. When the Major put in a few warm-up laps behind the Massey Harris motor, MacFarland settled in behind him.

The first match was over a mile, behind pacers. When the gun went off Corbett and Burton led them away, with Taylor and

MacFarland bringing up the rear. For the first two laps there was no change in positions. The crowd was tense and by all accounts watched in near total silence. On the third lap Corbett pulled out and Burton took over the pacing. Taylor still led MacFarland. On the fourth lap Burton dropped out half way around. Suddenly Taylor ran high on the bank at the Aquarium corner as though inviting MacFarland to go to the front. But Floyd didn't take him up on the offer. The Major came down to the inside again and led at the bell. The pace was still relatively easy.

Suddenly, with a mighty kick, MacFarland drew level on the outside and both men raced neck and neck at tremendous speed. Roar upon roar erupted from the audience as the riders soared into the corner.

Through the curve MacFarland steadily pulled away until a length separated him from the Major. As they came out and headed down the straight the crowd awaited Taylor's famous jump. If it came it was undetectable amid the high-speed sprinting. MacFarland, on the inside, powered over the finish line half a length ahead. The race had been two minutes and nine seconds of acute tension and the finish was deafening in its release for the audience, which cheered for a full half minute before the noise begin to subside. As Taylor later admitted, 'he defeated me fairly and squarely'.

The second race, also a mile, was to be unpaced. It was simply the two men against each other to the finish. When the two were pushed off MacFarland went to the lead and pedalled strongly for the first lap with Taylor trailing close behind. Floyd expected Taylor to then take his turn at the lead. Taylor didn't. MacFarland immediately slowed his pace and moved high up on the track on the western turn. Taylor slowed with him. Floyd slowed even more, until he was barely moving.

The race became an exhibition of trick riding. Who could

go the slowest and force his opponent to take the lead? Major Taylor was an expert at it. As one journalist wrote, 'he can crawl, stand still, go astern and generally cavort as though standing on shoe leather'. MacFarland did not buy into the game. He reached up, grabbed an electric light post, and stopped, looking back at Taylor.

The Australian crowd gazed in astonishment. In the midst of a match race between two of the best and most antagonistic cyclists in the world, one was stolidly holding onto a post in the glare of a 2,000 candle power arc light while the other was performing a balancing feat just behind. Finally Taylor reached over and grabbed the fence. Then the humour of it registered and laughter quickly rippled around the ground as the crowd released tension. After a few more seconds of 'fencing' MacFarland let go and headed down the bank with Taylor right behind.

It looked as if the race was resuming but the referee would not have a bar of it. He whistled the men back to the starting line. As Taylor rode into position his back tyre deflated and another machine was sent for. In the meantime MacFarland sat down next to the judges' enclosure. He exclaimed, 'It's not fair. The conditions are that we pace one another. I wasn't going to let him have my wheel and then jump me on the post'.

When the two men were pushed off for the re-start there was a perfect understanding with respect to pacing and with mechanical precision the two exchanged positions every half lap. At each change there was a roar from the crowd as they anticipated one or the other making a move. Neither did. On the fourth lap Taylor suddenly ran wide on the eastern bank. The crowd strained. It was expecting his jump, but nothing happened. As they crossed the start/finish line on the bell lap MacFarland took off. He was clearly going to try to outrace Taylor to the finish line. As one observer commented, he was 'grim determination'.

Melbourne Exhibition
Ground cycle track

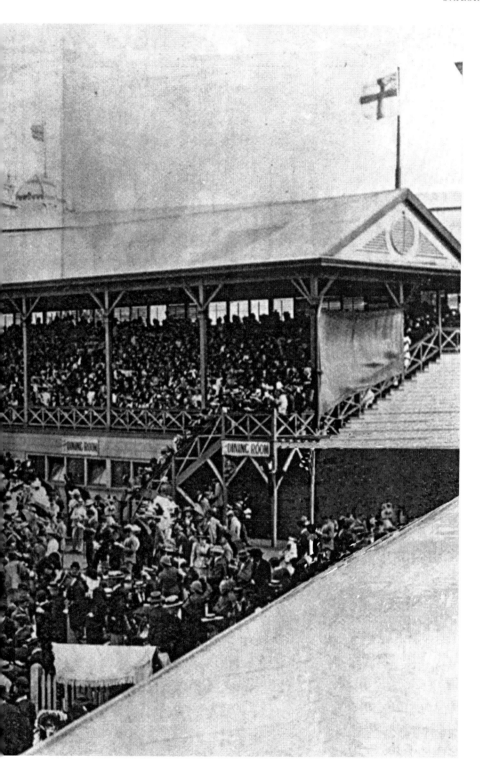

At headlong speed the competitors rode as MacFarland maintained his lead of over a length. Around the course and into the last straight a desperate battle ensued. Taylor drew up on his adversary's wheel, dropped back a good length, then hurled himself forward. But MacFarland was only ten yards from the finish. The crowd screamed relentlessly. The pistol fired and the race was over: 'So exciting a lap has never been ridden before'.

MacFarland passed the post, waved his hand gleefully in the air, and beamed as the delighted crowd frantically cheered him. Taylor wiped sweat from the end of his nose as he shot past MacFarland, a result of the speed he'd been travelling at the finish. Part way around the track the two again drew level. Floyd held out his left hand. The Major took it with his right and shook. The pair rode around that way, the crowd cheering. As they pedalled off the track the verdict was hoisted.

The spectators, stunned, looked at the board, the officials and one another. As one journalist commented, '19,997 men and women said MacFarland and turned over the programme for the next event'. But three—the judges—ruled otherwise. The race had been declared a dead heat. From the spectators came yells of rage, abuse, bad language and threats of personal violence. The crowd, in its anger, was on the verge of getting out of control.

One of the judges, Mr. Cuddigan, later gave his account. 'Five yards from the mark MacFarland was leading by a wheel but Taylor was going at twice the speed. At every revolution of his wheels he was perceptively gaining. Both crossed the mark simultaneously. MacFarland's head and neck were over the mark first, but we only judge by the wheels. Taylor's last kick did it. His sprint was wonderful'. George Broadbent, noted map maker, former cycle racer, and a highly respected man in Victorian cycling circles, was sitting immediately behind the judges. He concurred with the verdict: 'Taylor's last five yards were simply astounding'. The crowd disagreed, however, and let the judges know it. Throughout the remaining races that night the fans yelled 'dead heat', 'dead heat' at every finish, even if won by lengths.

What an evening. Taylor defeated in the first race, the second race brought to an ignominious standstill high on the bank, and then the re-start ending in a dead heat. What would happen next? Several other races were ridden while MacFarland and Taylor retired for a brief rest before resuming. Suddenly, and unexpectedly, the referee, Mr W. Gleeson, called together the press. He announced that there would be no further racing that night. It seems Floyd MacFarland had left the premises.

As the band struck up the anthem to signal the closing of activities, the crowd, now aware of events, swarmed over the fence and into the arena. Some of them confronted the judges and the language got offensive but the officials wisely held their peace. Eventually the ground emptied. The authorities consulted into the early morning hours. It was decided to finish the Taylor–MacFarland match immediately after the Taylor–Lawson match, the following Wednesday.

It would be a night to remember.

EXHIBITION OVAL.

———

TO MORROW NIGHT.

———

THE GREATEST PROGRAMME
IN POINT OF INTEREST
EVER PRESENTED TO A
SPORT-LOVING PUBLIC.

———

A GRAND FAREWELL
DOUBLE-BILL NIGHT.

———

MAJOR TAYLOR V. IVER LAWSON,
£150 PURSE £150.
Three Heats—One Mile, Two Miles, and One Mile.
Each Heat to be Solidly Paced.

———

FLOYD MACFARLAND V. MAJOR TAYLOR.

———

NOTE—On account of the unsatisfactory termination to Saturday night's match between these
famous rivals, the L.V.W., the controlling body
of Victorian cycling, have definitely decided to
order the running of this match at this meeting,
and the governing conditions will be so rigidly
enforced that any further unpleasantness will be
totally avoided.

———

Gates open 6.30. First race, 7.30
ADMISSION, 1/; Stand, 1/ extra.

———

THOS. M. ROBERTSON, Secretary

*The Argus, 16th
February, 1904*

100

10. The Incident

By the time the Melbourne newspapers hit the streets on Monday the promoters had done their homework. Among the numerous articles analysing and criticising Saturday's races were advertisements touting the forthcoming Wednesday night meet. Acknowledging that the public did not like the MacFarland–Taylor stand-off on the banked turn, the promoters had arranged to have each event solidly paced. They also emphasised that it was a grand farewell double-bill night. Taylor, Lawson and MacFarland would not be seen again in Melbourne. That should bring in the crowds.

There had been a tremendous outcry over MacFarland walking off the grounds. His behaviour was a slap in the face of the paying public. Consequently the promoters pointedly noted that 'On account of the unsatisfactory termination to Saturday night's match between these famous rivals, the Victorian League of Wheelmen, the controlling body of Victorian cycling, have definitely decided to order the running of this match at this meeting and the governing conditions will be so rigidly enforced that any further unpleasantness will be totally avoided'. It was signed by Thomas Robertson, Secretary of the Victorian League of Wheelmen. It was a forceful statement, but one he was to rue.

Late Wednesday morning tensions soared in the League offices. MacFarland had just notified them that, owing to illness, he would not be able to start. Mr Mountain, the president of the Federal Cycling Council, together with Dr Black and Mr Gleeson, the referee, went directly to St Kilda and interviewed MacFarland. He was eating

The one-fifth mile Exhibition Ground track, showing light standards

a large meal and seemed fine. Was it a ploy by MacFarland? An attempt to affect gambling odds? A psychological strategy against the Major? Whatever the case the Victorian League of Wheelmen were not buying it. The officials were blunt. If one competitor, meaning MacFarland, refused to come out, the other, meaning Taylor, could simply ride over the course and win the match and the £225 prize money. The League was not about to be intimidated by the American giant.

That evening, February 17th, the weather was again delightful. Surprisingly, only 18,000 people showed to see the Major take on both MacFarland and Lawson in deciding match races. But the excitement was no less intense, egged on, as one newspaper put it, 'by insinuous newspaper advertisements'. During one of the preliminary races three riders fell at the Aquarium corner. A fourth crashed into them, turned a complete somersault off his machine and was carried out on a stretcher.

Prior to their confrontation with Major Taylor both Lawson and MacFarland rode in a five-mile scratch race. With the exception of the Major and Don Walker all of the top riders in the country were involved. With 14 laps to go two Australians dashed ahead amid a roar from the crowd. MacFarland, considering that almost an impertinence, in 'a few mighty kicks' not only bridged the gap but put a quarter of a lap between himself and the entire field. Then, with a grin on his face, he slowed up until the pack closed. With one lap left MacFarland and Lawson sprinted away from the others. It was not a bad effort for a sick man.

At 8:30 the first of the Taylor–Lawson heats was run. The crowd cheered as the two men came on the track. The paced one-miler was fast and the champions followed with machine-like precision. At the bell there was not the slightest attempt at finesse. Away sprinted Lawson with Taylor hot on his wheels. Taylor rapidly pulled

PERFORMANCES OF

Iver Lawson

RAN second to Kramer on points last season in America. Kramer scored 62 and Lawson 50. Macfarland was third with 21.

Recent performances in America :—

Beat Kramer in Ten-Mile Professional Handicap.

* * *

Australia.

First in One-Mile Handicap, 15 yards behind scratch.

First in Five-Mile Scratch—11 min. 4 4·5 sec.

First in Ten-Mile Scratch—22 min. 14 2·5 sec.

First in Australian Handicap, one mile, 15 yards behind scratch—1 min. 55 2·5 sec.

First in Orient Plate, one mile, at Sydney.

First in Stuart Mile at Melbourne.

First in Invitation Scratch at Melbourne.

First in One and Ten Mile A.N.A. Gold Stakes.

First in heat of One-Mile A.N.A. Gold Stakes.

Third in Five-Mile A.N.A. Gold Stakes.

First in McCullagh Plate at Sydney, five miles. Record time, 10 min 57 2·5 sec.

First in second distance of International Test.

First in Adelaide Handicap, half-mile. Record time for Sydney, 54 3·5 sec.

First in Half-Mile Handicap at Coolgardie. Record time for the Goldfields, 57 1·5 sec.

First in grand final A.N.A. Gold Stakes.

First in Half-mile International Scratch at Melbourne.

First in Five mile International Scratch at Melbourne.

Floyd Macfarland,

RIGHTLY known as " The World's Handicap King."

Most recent victories in America :—

First Ten-Mile Professional Race. Time, 23 min. 29 2·5 sec.

First in final of Championship Race.

* * *

In Australia.

First in Ellegaard Scratch, five miles, at Sydney.

First in Open Handicap, one mile, at Melbourne—1 min. 58 sec.

Third International Scratch at Melbourne

First International Mile at Melbourne.

First in Westral Wheel Race at Coolgardie.

First in One-Mile, Two-Mile, and Five-Mile at Melbourne.

First in One-Mile Handicap at Sydney.

First in heat of League Handicap, starting 20 yards behind scratch.

First in Macfarland Plate, five miles.

Beat Major Taylor in one-mile match, first heat ; dead heat in the second heat.

First in Northcote Stakes, Adelaide.

First in Five-mile Scratch, Adelaide.

First in Sir E. T. Smith Stakes, Adelaide.

GRIMBLEY'S HOTEL,
Brighton Beach.

Two Large Dining Rooms. Wines, Spirits, &c., of the best. Large Room for Smoke Nights. The Cyclists' Rendezvous. Visitors will receive every attention.

J. R. Cathie, Proprietor.

The Australian Cyclist and Motor-car World, *25th February, 1904*

alongside and they raced shoulder-to-shoulder for half a lap. Then Taylor slowly crept away. At the finish line he led by three lengths and was riding easily, sitting up. It was his third straight man-on-man victory over Lawson.

The second match between Major Taylor and Iver Lawson

was over two miles, paced by Ben Goodson, Burton and Steve Gordon. As the three pacers set off Taylor settled in tightly behind them with Lawson bringing up the rear. The pace was fast and steady. At the bell lap the last pacer dropped out leaving Taylor and Lawson alone on the track. Taylor quickly sprinted away but Lawson rode hard and soon pulled level. On the back straight they bumped several times, at great speed. As they charged into the Aquarium corner the two suddenly collided. Taylor was thrown violently to the track.

Horrified groans burst from the crowd. Lawson kept his balance and swept across the finish line. Back on the track Taylor lay motionless and Dr Macgillicuddy rushed towards him. The crowd's mood changed radically and there was a storm of booing hurled at Lawson as he slowly wound down around the track; he was quickly escorted to the dressing room. Dr Macgillicuddy and a small group huddled about the Major. After several more minutes he was lifted up and with assistance limped towards his room. He was severely

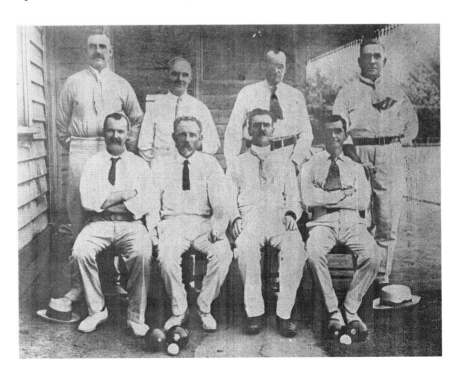

Dr Macgillicuddy (front row, second from right)

shaken, bruised and bleeding from cuts on his thigh and arm. He did not look well. It was possibly the worst fall of Taylor's career.

Within minutes the stewards declared the heat a 'no race'. Over the next hour other races were run to fill in time as Macgillicuddy attended to Taylor. Eventually the doctor sent word to the stewards to run yet another event. Officials added a couple of more races. By 10:20 in the evening Taylor had still not appeared

Then out on the track strode the giant, Floyd MacFarland, in his gown. He simply stood there, waiting, saying nothing. That very afternoon officials of the Victorian League of Wheelmen had given MacFarland the ultimatum: If one did not ride and the other did, he could claim the prize money. *MacFarland* now was prepared to race, but *Taylor* was unavailable. This was not quite what the officials had anticipated. The situation was tense.

All eyes turned to the grandstand and the officials' box. After a few minutes consultation they called for another race while further discussions were held. When that race ended the band struck up and simultaneously a strong contingent of police suddenly appeared on the track. The spectators filed out in near silence. As they did so the officials declared the Taylor–Lawson and Taylor–MacFarland matches 'postponed indefinitely'.

The promoters had their lucre, but it was tarnished. The Melbourne *Argus* declared the meetings a 'cycling fiasco'; the matches were unfinished; it did not appear that the Major would be able to ride for some time; he had lodged a formal complaint against Iver Lawson for interference; and Floyd MacFarland had lodged a formal demand for his money because the Major failed to come on to the track. For the Victorian League of Wheelmen it was a nightmare. It was hard to imagine any worse outcome from the great Battle of the Champions.

The Battle of Champions

**A Disappointing Evening. Dissatisfied Crowd.
Lawson-Taylor Match Unfinished. Taylor Laid Out.
Was It Intentional?
Stewards' Investigation. Macfarland-Taylor Match Postponed.
Macfarland Claims the Stake. Police Prevent Disturbance.
Lawson Disqualified for Twelve Months.**

A Cycling Crisis

There is no disputing the fact that we are passing through a severe cycling Crisis, out of which the sport will ultimately emerge with draggled feathers. The great match contests about which almost everyone raved, have become a by-word and a reproach in the minds of the public, and it is certain that a great revulsion of popular feeling has set in towards them. By an unfortuitous set of circumstances, the members of the L.V.W., in connection with these matches, have incurred the opprobrium of the public. It was well known that they were divided in regard to the question of patronage, and it was rumoured that bribes had been offered in connection with the matter. On top of that a decision was given which the people declare to be the outcome of favouritism: Macfarland practically defies the L.V.W.; Taylor is injured; the match ends in a *fiasco*, and the public are disgusted and sickened.

The Australian Cyclist and Motor-Car World, *February 25, 1904*

108

11. Inquiry and Aftermath

It was time for firm and decisive action, without delay. That very night the stewards took preliminary evidence at the track. They also ordered the prize money to be held by the Victorian League of Wheelmen pending the outcome of the investigation. Throughout the next day a Committee of Inquiry interviewed various riders and officials. They took statements and asked questions. The fundamental issue was whether Iver Lawson deliberately caused Major Taylor's crash.

The testimony and the committee's discussions were never made public. However, newspaper reports of comments made by many participants give a clear indication of the tenor. Taylor stated categorically that he was deliberately thrown by Lawson. Lawson, whose riding career could be at stake depending on the severity of punishment, was more extensive in his explanation. 'The only thing I can say about it is that Taylor's fall was his own fault. Everybody who saw it seems to think so. When he collided, I felt as if he tried to push me up the bank. People have since told me that he attempted to shove me off'.

MacFarland readily offered not only his opinion of who was at fault but the penalty they should suffer. 'Look here, if any other rider had done what Taylor did, he would have gone under for a year. At the time he fell he was beaten. Lawson was about three-quarters of a length past him and Taylor reached out and pushed Lawson up the bank so that he could get through on the inside, then he struck his pedal on the bank and dropped'.

The Victorian League of Wheelmen's officials stationed nearest the accident asserted that the collision was intentional.

Forty-eight hours after the race the stewards were still huddled together. At 1:00 am Saturday morning they came out of their chambers and announced their decision. There was 'deliberate intent' on Lawson's part and he was disqualified for a year. Since the Victorian League was party to both Australian and international agreements it meant that Lawson would effectively be unable to race anywhere in the world, a severe blow to a man of his stature and income. Nonetheless, some believed that if Lawson were guilty of deliberate intent then the sentence was in fact 'paltry'. The Sydney *Worker* felt that Lawson had engaged in a 'murderous and cowardly business'. As another journalist commented, 'The enormity of such a crime could only be compensated by a "lifer"'.

After giving his testimony Lawson had boarded a train to Adelaide where he was to race on Saturday. It was there that he heard about his disqualification. He was not allowed to ride and immediately returned to Melbourne to appeal. The basic ground upon which he would contest his case was that he had not deliberately fouled Taylor. Several journalists, from their view from the press table, agreed with him. *The Australian Cyclist*'s representative felt that Lawson, seeing Taylor so close up and fearing a collision, made a spring, hoping to get away; in his excitement his knee struck Taylor's handlebar and Taylor fell. Lawson himself was adamant: 'I absolutely deny that there was any intention on my part to foul Taylor'. One reporter summed up the dilemma: 'After all, who is able to prove it? The whole thing was over in a flash and at the most only two officials saw the occurrence at close range'. In that pre-video replay era it was a powerful argument.

Later in life Taylor wrote that his trainer, Sid Melville, had passed on advice to him from other Australian trainers to watch out for some 'dirty-work'. MacFarland had reportedly laid a lot of money

This building, originally a residence, was later reopened as the Port Phillip Club Hotel, a popular venue for various Melbourne sporting clubs and organisations

on Iver and told him that if he could not beat Taylor, then he would have to 'throw' him in order to protect the money. If the Major gave similar testimony at the Inquiry and Appeal, and any sort of corroboration was obtained from anyone else, it would have made Lawson's case difficult.

An eight-man Appeal Board eventually examined 20 witnesses in the course of two sittings at the Port Phillip Club Hotel. They finally retired to consider their finding, reached a decision within an hour, and called in Lawson. 'The Board, not being fully satisfied after hearing all the evidence on both sides, that the fall of Taylor was brought about by the deliberate intention of Lawson, still considers that the latter was guilty of unfair and careless riding and in the circumstances have determined that a disqualification of three months will meet the case and therefore reduces the term fixed by the stewards to the said period'. In effect they told Lawson that he wasn't wanted in Australia anymore that season, but by the time he caught a boat abroad and did some training he would be able to participate in the northern hemisphere summer, including the world cycling championships in London.

The Appeal Board had attempted to tread a fine line for the League while cycling administrators in general were under intense pressure from the public and press. Many were getting tired of the unfair riding against Taylor. They were also angry at some of the wrist-slaps administered for past infringements, especially MacFarland's early season suspension being remitted to a £25 fine, which had conveniently allowed him to make appearances at a number of important meets. Unlike in New South Wales, where the syndicate's head, McIntosh, was Secretary of the League Council, none of the Victorian League members was involved in the tour promotion per se. Thus there was not the same internal pressure. The Appeal Board's compromise was thought wise by many.

Others, however, were still unhappy. In particular, a number of the League's members had voted against granting League patronage to the matches in the first place because they distrusted the promoters. Rumours abounded that bribes had been offered to obtain the League's support. A special meeting had been called and the issue hotly debated. Grudgingly the dissidents withdrew their opposition and the races were allowed to proceed under the League's auspices. However, the matches' inconclusiveness rekindled the dissension. In accepting the inability to prove Lawson's intent to foul, and yet ruling that he had ridden recklessly, the Board had tried to salvage some respectability from the whole morass. They had not entirely succeeded. As the public and press over the next several weeks attacked the general state of cycling, the League's name frequently appeared in print, tarred by the promoters and feathered by the public.

❖❖❖

The cycling circus moved on to Adelaide where three separate days of racing were scheduled. The first was on Saturday, February 20th, only three days after the Melbourne contretemps. On Thursday *The Advertiser* said that the meet 'promised to be one of the most largely attended ever conducted here'. On Friday they optimistically reported that Taylor was fit to ride. However, on Saturday they notified their readers, sadly, that Taylor could not make it for that day's meet. Back in Melbourne the Major was reclining on a settee in his room, nursing his injuries. Aside from bruises he had suffered painful lacerations on his forearm and thigh. He certainly hoped to be well enough to mount the saddle again soon but the Adelaide trip was out.

By the time of the meet word had also got around that Lawson had been disqualified and would not be participating. He asked a journalist to 'tell the Adelaide people that I'm sorry to have disappointed them'. The following week he took a train to Sydney and from there a boat back to America, 'more than pleased' with the financial results in Australia.

The result was that of the great American triumvirate only MacFarland was on view in Adelaide. That was not enough to entice large numbers to part with their shillings. The gate takings for the day were only £208. Interestingly, in a rare omission, the papers did not report the attendance. However, as there are 20 shillings to the pound, and assuming a thousand paid extra to sit in the grandstand, probably no more than 3,000 people showed up. Things did not look good for next Wednesday's week day meet.

Mr George Ruthven, Secretary of the South Australian League of Wheelmen, took one look at the situation and boarded the next train for Melbourne to consult with his Victorian counterparts. He wanted Iver Lawson at the Adelaide meeting and tried to convince the Victorian League to remove Lawson's disqualification. As one Victorian journalist wrote, 'Could impudence go farther? Unless I am much mistaken, Mr Ruthven will find he has come to the wrong shop with such an outrageous request'. Whatever other pressures were brought to bear on the Victorian League of Wheelmen this was not one they needed.

George Ruthven

They refused to whitewash Lawson for the sake of their South Australian brethren. Mr Ruthven returned home empty handed.

On Wednesday things were even worse in Adelaide than predicted. Floyd MacFarland won all the major races and pedalled his victory laps to the tune of 'Yankee Doodle', but the total takings were £73. Including the riders and officials, there could not have been more than 1,000 people present. When the news of the Adelaide attendance figures got back to Sydney and Melbourne there was only one possible conclusion. The tour was in deep trouble.

The cycling fraternity and promoters had no one to blame but themselves. The 'great revenge matches' in Melbourne had backfired. The 'insinuating' advertisements promised sensationalism and delivered it—but not as intended. As a Melbourne journalist wrote, 'Many of the crowd, not seeing that for which they had come, left the ground shrugging their shoulders with the intention of never going again'. His view was that 'The presence of the world's [best] cyclists would tend to do injury to cycle racing by too rapidly developing an inordinate craving for sensationalism in the minds of the people; a craving which would, through being pampered, eat itself down to the bitter end in a season or two'. He was right but his timing was wrong. It looked as if it would not take even the rest of the current season.

With The Sydney Thousand just over a month away matters looked very dark. A newspaper reported that Taylor was more seriously injured than was at first supposed and it might be three weeks before he could mount a bicycle again. One could be forgiven for imagining the members of the South Australian League of Wheelmen and the Sydney Summer Nights Amusement Committee at that point dropping on their knees in collective prayer, beseeching a miracle.

One was delivered to them on February 27th in Adelaide.

*Major Taylor with
Sid Melville at the
Adelaide Oval*

116

12. The Adelaide Episode

Major Taylor, still recuperating from his injuries, was as aware as anyone of the plight of the Adelaide races. When George Ruthven went to Melbourne to discuss the Lawson disqualification he had paid a call on the Major, imploring him to come to South Australia if at all possible. After returning to Adelaide, Ruthven continued to send wires back to Taylor inquiring as to his condition and whether he would be coming.

The Major had a special fondness in his heart for the city and its people, for they had been particularly gracious and welcoming the previous year. He felt he owed them something. Taylor's wife and Dr Macgillicuddy counselled against it but Taylor decided to go. He notified the South Australian officials that he was coming and when Friday night's train left Melbourne for Adelaide he was aboard. It was a sleepless night as he was still bothered by the injuries. When the train arrived in the morning the Major went directly to the Adelaide Oval. The newspapers' announcements of his appearance had the desired effect. By race time there were 20,000 people around the track.

Taylor had not been on a bicycle since the crash, 10 days before. He went out behind the grandstand with his trainer and removed the bandages. Sid Melville helped him aboard the machine. His injured, extended right leg rested on the pedal, in its lowest position. Sid slowly rocked the fixed wheel bicycle back and forth, increasing the swing of the pedal until Taylor was able to make a complete revolution. In the process, some of the skin over the cut broke and blood began to ooze again, but the Major was able to move his leg

Iver Lawson, banned from riding (in suit) is on the left. The mounted cyclists (left to right) are Hardy Downing, Floyd MacFarland and Orlando Stevens.

surprisingly easily. He stuck cotton on the bleeding and rolled onto the track. The crowd gave Taylor a thunderous ovation as he settled down for a several mile pedal. After the light workout he retired to his tent for a rub-down. He felt 'fit and confident'.

The organisers had placed him, at his request, in a slow heat early in the program as a try-out. It went well. The crowd appreciated Taylor's effort in riding in even a moderately paced race and gave him a rousing cheer. Later he qualified in his official heat for the mile championship.

Few expected much of Taylor in the big race, including Taylor himself. With the exception of Iver Lawson all the best were at Adelaide. But what happened next was one of those things that, occasionally in sporting history, transcends the moment. The source can be anger, revenge, inspiration, or the desire to prove something to oneself or to others. Whatever the cause, onlookers witness—and competitors are subjected to—a remarkable performance. It happened because the Major broke a hitherto fundamental principle that he loudly proclaimed and to which he had unwaveringly adhered.

Most chapters in Major Taylor's autobiography typically open with one or two brief paragraphs by the Major, followed by several pages of verbatim reproduction of newspaper articles. To be generous about it, it can be dull reading. A notable exception is the chapter on the Adelaide race, where five of the six pages were written by Taylor himself. Having been produced some 25 years after the fact there are inaccuracies, but he does provide us with his own view of what happened. When matched with newspaper accounts of the day it reveals a fundamental lesson about human beings. There can come a time in life when enough is enough.

Taylor lay in his tent being massaged by the trainer when the West Australian rider, Bill MacDonald, charged in, angry. MacFarland, up to his old tricks, had convened a group of riders to discuss a plan to ensure that Major Taylor did not win. An injured Taylor notwithstanding, Floyd was taking no chances. There was nothing new in such arrangements, of course, but what was new was that for the first time in his Australian tour the Major was an outright underdog. It was seen as a gallant and respected effort by him to come to the Adelaide Oval, injured and sore as he was. As Australians would put it, if the Major was willing to 'give it a go' in his circumstances, then 'give him a fair go'. But Floyd MacFarland was not an Australian.

Bill MacDonald

119

Capacity crowd at a cricket match at the Adelaide Oval, January 1904. Three months later, Taylor raced before a crowd of this size

In the context of handicap bicycle racing, the combinations were acceptable, in the eyes of many, if all the riders knew the score, picked their teams, and raced accordingly. If Major Taylor elected of his own accord to put himself above and beyond it all, so be it. He was his own man, a team of one. It could all be justified. Bill MacDonald, the alleged principal culprit in preventing Taylor from winning his heat and making it to the finals of the Sydney Thousand the previous year, could not justify in his own mind what was happening that day, however. He offered to help the Major in whatever way he could. Taylor thanked him for his sportsmanship but said, in effect, 'no thanks' and asked MacDonald not to do anything rash. As Bill started to leave the tent Taylor disingenuously threw off a parting shot. 'If you really want to see me bring that bunch into camp, all I want you to do is go to the last lap at top speed, and be sure to hold the black line [the pole position] all the way, regardless of what position I am in'.

The starter sent the field on its way. Hunt and Gordon set an uneventful but quick early pace, with Major Taylor behind, followed

by the others. The speed gradually picked up. At the start of the bell lap MacDonald suddenly jumped into the lead and Taylor followed behind him. Almost immediately Hardy Downing drew alongside MacDonald, on the outside, and MacFarland and Fred Scheps moved directly behind Downing, trapping Taylor in a pocket.

As MacDonald and Downing battled side by side down the

Taylor (arrowed), trapped in a pocket

back stretch and charged into the final turn, MacFarland saw his chance. He pulled to the outside and sprinted past the pair. It was a beautifully executed manoeuvre as the tightly bunched field swept around the long northern end of the oval. The crowd roared when MacFarland made his break, then the roar redoubled. MacDonald, on the inside, had moved out slightly. Major Taylor shot through underneath and came out of the turn just inches ahead of MacFarland. Taylor not only held off MacFarland but extended his lead to three quarters of a length. He swept over the line to victory with 20,000 fans cheering him.

(Right and facing page)
Floyd MacFarland in Adelaide

MacFarland with Sir Edwin Smith, prior to Taylor's arrival in Adelaide

Major Taylor called it 'the greatest personal victory' of his life. But the victory wasn't achieved alone. He had help and MacFarland knew it. Floyd rode over the line with his hand raised in protest but got no sympathy. The crowd hooted him as he pedalled across the grass to the referee's table. He was waved away.

Taylor rode his lap of honour to a tumultuous uproar and applause. Old Glory flew alongside the Australian and British flags on the grandstand and the band played the 'Stars and Stripes Forever'. When Taylor climbed off his wheel he 'trembled with emotion' and his trainer, Sid Melville, was ecstatic. It was for Taylor 'the most thrilling episode' of his career.

Meanwhile MacFarland stormed around the track in a rage, talking to anyone who would listen—other officials, reporters, and 'even to the bandsmen'. In the end 'he made a needless exhibition of himself and convinced the public of the bitterness of the rivalry between himself and Taylor.' He threatened to 'get the Major' in the next race, a five-miler. However, Taylor, in his condition, had already informed the promoters he wouldn't be riding again. MacFarland, stymied and vindictive, burst out at a reporter 'He's a fine game nigger; he won't come out in this race'. Taylor said that he 'did not desire to make any statements that would cause friction'. And his views of the pocketing incident? 'People have good eyes and don't know how to use them'.

The Major was wrong. A lot of people knew how to use their eyes, most of all the other cyclists, and they knew what they had seen. Taylor had made an 'arrangement'. As one journalist observed several days later, the riders 'are not done talking about it yet'. The implications were enormous. In one month The Sydney Thousand would be held with a £750 first prize. If the Major were to team with someone in that race ...

With his out-of-character, totally unexpected turn of events the Major had, in one fell swoop, set a black cat among the white pigeons.

Sellout Crowd at Sydney Cricket Ground

13. The Sydney Thousand

Adelaide may have been the Major's greatest thrill, it may have been deeply satisfying to the crowd, and it may have stunned his co-riders, but international reputations weren't made in Adelaide. That could only be done in the high-priced pressure-cooker that was the Sydney Cricket Ground. There was found the Holy Grail of Australasia's cyclists in 1904, and several Americans had come to worship.

The Sydney Thousand. Three magic words that stood for wealth and cycling fame. As soon as the world's richest race finished, details of the event would begin pulsing out of the Sydney telegraph office to the cycling centres of the world. They would be read in Paris and Brussels and Amsterdam and Copenhagen and London and New York. If a hitherto obscure Australian or New Zealander should manage to win he would achieve instant international recognition. It could open doors that might otherwise remain forever closed. It was the stuff of dreams with a setting to match. The SCG was spectacular with its brilliantly illuminated stands and lawns. When the grandstand electric lights were turned off at the start of each race, the gas lit track, with its fast-moving wheelmen, was compelling.

The Sydney Summer Nights Amusement Committee put its publicity machine in full gear. In one promotional effort they offered cheques worth anywhere from 10 shillings to £5 each to people lucky enough be displaying one of the 18 secretly marked handbills of the upcoming race. Thousands of Sydneysiders posted them in their residential and business windows. *The Sydney Sportsman* predicted the racing excitement would make a 'sensitive person's hair fairly stand on end'.

Gaslight on the track and electric light in the stands at the Sydney Cricket Ground

The Sydney Thousand was a-one mile handicap race held over two nights. The final would be run on Wednesday, the 23rd. On the first night, in mid-March, there was a series of qualifying heats. MacFarland and Taylor won theirs easily. The big race that night was the Kent Plate, a one-mile handicap. It brought Taylor and MacFarland together for the first time since their Adelaide encounter, along with Hardy Downing and Don Walker. Each of the four had a pace rider. When the starter sent them off Taylor quickly moved to the front and shouted to his pacer to speed it up. At the bell lap Taylor had a substantial lead and appeared on his way to a solid victory. Suddenly MacFarland, in a brilliant sprint, shot by him and powered across the line a half length ahead. MacFarland savoured his victory and circled the track twice to loud cheers and a continuing ovation while Taylor admitted to reporters that he had been fairly beaten.

Who *was* the better man of the two? There simply seemed to be no answer. Taylor had come out of bed to convincingly beat MacFarland just two weeks before, and yet tonight Floyd had clearly surpassed him in riding and tactical skills. On the Exhibition Track in Melbourne Taylor had been cleanly beaten by MacFarland in the first race and, although the second was declared a dead heat, many felt that the Major had lost that as well. Clearly Taylor felt he had to prove himself the better of the two. The situation was so disturbing that he offered to undertake a series of man-to-man races between himself and Floyd. Money was not the issue as he was willing to ride five races for a total £100 purse, winner take all. The price of pride had suddenly dropped.

Negotiations proved extremely difficult. While the two riders agreed in principle that it would be a best-of-five match races, the arguing point was what the five races would be. Taylor wanted them to be short. MacFarland, known and respected for his stamina, wanted them long. Finally it was agreed that MacFarland and Taylor would each select two events, and McIntosh would specify the fifth race. MacFarland chose a pursuit race to open the series, each man starting from opposite sides of the track, followed by a one-mile race, paced by single riders, *on the condition that it would have to have a time limit of one minute and 50 seconds*. The Sydney sports writers were dumbfounded. That was only one second over his mile record of one minute 49 seconds. Nonetheless Taylor agreed and specified a quarter-mile and half-mile race, each paced by single riders. McIntosh chose an unpaced mile for the fifth race. The matches were arranged for the Saturday and Monday following The Sydney Thousand. A full program of events was drawn up around the challenge matches.

What a remarkable state of affairs for the promoters. Just one month before the tour looked in tatters. Lawson was suspended, Taylor was injured, and the remaining cyclists were pedalling around the Adelaide Oval before a £73 crowd. What they now had was Taylor's stunning upset of MacFarland in Adelaide; MacFarland's striking defeat of the Major in the Kent Plate; the prospect of a turn-away crowd in a few days at the final of The Sydney Thousand; and two days of Taylor-MacFarland man-on-man match races coming up—at a bargain rate of £100 prize money. Those warm evenings on the shores of Sydney Harbour in late March, 1904 must have felt lovely indeed for the members of the Sydney Summer Nights Amusement Committee.

❖ ❖ ❖

If the 1904 Australian cycling season had been dreamed up by a Hollywood screen writer it could hardly have been better. An exotic setting. A black American hero with a lovely wife who had overcome all odds and the 'monster prejudice' to become the world's best at his business. A white American arch-villain who, in the best David and Goliath tradition, towered over the hero by 9 inches, was a master manipulator of men, and a great athlete in his own right. A coterie of talented sub-villains, including a soon-to-be world champion, and a gang of opportunistic promoters. Action aplenty in the form of spectacular races, attempted race fixing, and man-to-man showdowns that proved utterly inconclusive. A dastardly deed on the track. The hero climbing out of bed to defeat the arch-villain against all expectations. An Australian villain who suddenly has a turn of heart and becomes a good guy. The hero's dilemma in having to decide whether to bend, if not break, one of his guiding principles. And throughout, the all-white crowds barracking the black hero in his rides against the odds.

How does one end such a scenario? If a screen writer were given the brief, what would he write? He might come up with what was about to actually happen. But it's doubtful.

❖ ❖ ❖

On the Wednesday night of The Sydney Thousand final over 30,000 people, 'having to hang onto trams like bees', converged on the Sydney Cricket Ground. Six per cent of the city's half million population watched the Minister for Public Works ceremoniously fire the gas lights around the track, and the preliminary races were run. Of 90 original entrants for the big race, only 11 were left. They pedalled onto the track, did a few warm-up laps and then took their places. Taylor and MacFarland, the back-markers, were side-by-side. Ten yards ahead was Hardy Downing. Don Walker was another 10 yards further along. Ten yards past him was Fred Scheps from South Australia. They made up the back bunch. Between 100 and 200 yards down the track were six more riders who would form the front bunch, Corbett, Plunkett, Gordon, O'Brien, Bathie and Kett. That group was fast. Indeed, many felt that Larry Corbett's 120-yard handicap was the edge he needed. Bettors had made him 2-1 odds-on favourite to win. Taylor was at 3-1 against, MacFarland 6-1 against.

The riders' front wheels were on their marks, their feet strapped to the pedals, an official behind each, balancing them. The 'starter's whistle struck every ear with startling clearness'. The riders tensed. A second later the starter's gun exploded and simultaneously

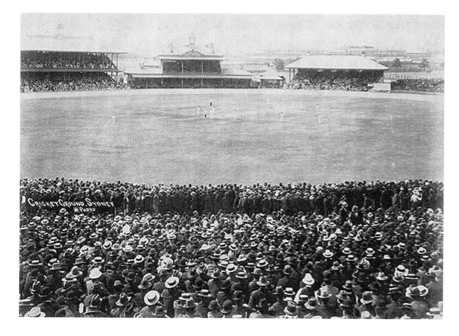

SCG spectators

the grandstand electric lights went black. Eleven machines leapt forward under the stark glare of the track lights. The crowd erupted in a cheer. One minute and 54 seconds later it would be over. It was not only a rich race, but was going to be a very fast one.

Taylor shot off the mark, closed the 10-yard gap on Downing almost immediately, and passed him. MacFarland also bolted around him and closed on Taylor's wheel. The trio set out after Walker just ahead, who himself was making a strong effort to catch Scheps. In the front bunch the riders had also began closing on one another.

The Sydney Thousand rapidly developed into a classic of handicap racing. The front bunch, pacing one another, was flying around the track as the back bunch tried to overhaul them. It looked as if they would be able to but it was not going to be easy. Indeed, as the race progressed it seemed that both groups might reach the finish line at virtually the same time.

At the bell, with one lap to go, Corbett, Plunkett and O'Brien were bunched together at the front. Thirty yards back followed Taylor, MacFarland and Walker. The fierce pace had taken its toll and the other five riders had dropped out. Among the back trio Walker had more than carried his share of the pacing. He was tired and trailing. Taylor, having paced for some distance, now pulled out wide to allow MacFarland to take the final lead. It was getting desperate. There was less than a lap to go and still a 30-yard gap lay ahead. MacFarland refused to take over. Taylor hesitated only momentarily and then reassumed the pacing chore. As they headed into the next banked turn Taylor again pulled wide for MacFarland. MacFarland rode high on the bank and again refused to take the lead. Moments before they had been within striking distance of the front bunch, now it became apparent that they weren't going to close the gap.

In the front bunch Plunkett led Corbett and O'Brien down the back stretch at a blistering pace. Everyone now realised that the winner would come from this trio. As they charged into the final turn, Plunkett swung wide and Corbett shot through on the inside to take the lead, with O'Brien behind him. Plunkett immediately pulled back down alongside O'Brien, trapping him. As they swept out of the last turn, Plunkett momentarily fell back. As the trap opened, O'Brien took his opportunity. He swung out and charged after Corbett. The two sprinted fiercely for the finish line, the crowd screaming. Corbett swept across the line only inches ahead of O'Brien, with Plunkett a half-length back. An immense roar from the crowd was plainly heard 'for miles down the harbour'. Major Taylor was fourth, several yards behind. He had failed in a last ditch solo effort to close the gap on the front bunch. MacFarland was fifth, Walker a distant sixth. The other five did not finish.

Larry Corbett completed his victory lap and to great cheers was hoisted upon the shoulders of the throng. As one journalist noted, 'Only once before in the history of the world had the extraordinary spectacle of one man earning a prize of £750 on the racing track in less than two minutes been witnessed'. And this time it was a local hero.

The Australian Cyclist, published in Melbourne, came out on Thursday each week. Being the leading cycling journal of the nation the editor wanted to include a report of the premier cycling event of the season in the next day's issue. Immediately after the race his correspondent rushed off to telegraph his copy to Melbourne. It was brief but covered the essence. The writer concluded with the statement that 'To the accompaniment of the report of the pistol, The Sydney Thousand for 1904 becomes an annal of the past'.

He was wrong. Although the pedalling had just finished, the race for the prize money had only begun. A scandalous storm was about to erupt over The Sydney Thousand.

Council of the League, to Naughty-boy M'Farland : " Now, will you be good !"

The Sydney
Sportsman, *6 April
1904*

14. The Storm

As the cheering for Corbett abated it revealed underlying unease among the fans. Don Walker had done most of the pacing in helping the back trio to close the gap on the front bunch and Major Taylor the rest. MacFarland had contributed only a half-lap early on. Many felt that had MacFarland done his share he and Taylor would have been among the front bunch during the last lap. Rumblings of discontent echoed through the crowd and many began to hoot MacFarland.

Corbett had hardly begun celebrating his victory when Alfred O'Brien, the second place finisher, charged across the field to the stewards. He accused Corbett and Plunkett of collusion. He claimed that they had fought him for 30 yards down the back straight, running him onto the grass, and that subsequently Plunkett had bumped O'Brien, interfering with his chance of winning. He was furious.

The referee, Mr Wilkie, called together the stewards and McIntosh to discuss the matter. The two umpires in the vicinity of the incident were brought over. They said they had not seen any interference or collusion. Plunkett admitted that he and O'Brien had bumped, but it was only minor and purely accidental. He insisted that he had not interfered with O'Brien, had not kept him on the grass, and emphatically denied any collusion whatsoever between himself and Corbett. After extensive discussion the referee and stewards dismissed O'Brien's protest. The remaining spectators began leaving.

O'Brien, still intensely angry, marched over to the Council of New South Wales League of Wheelmen and lodged a formal appeal.

The Council acted immediately. It called various riders and took statements. A remnant crowd milled about. The hours dragged on, matters taking an ominous turn. Not only did the Council not reach a decision but it interviewed MacFarland and Taylor, who had not been anywhere near the alleged interference. The Council eventually announced that it would continue the inquiry later. In the meantime it withheld all prize money.

When the last people filed out of the Sydney Cricket Ground in the early morning hours, possibly only O'Brien had good cause for optimism. Even if the appeal was not upheld, he would still get £100. If it was, he stood to receive £750. That was well worth waiting for. Corbett, who hours before was at the peak of exhilaration, receiving the ovation of the crowd, went home empty handed.

The Council of the New South Wales League of Wheelmen met the next day in what turned out to be an extraordinary hearing. Instead of the customary simple statements, all witnesses were sworn, evidence taken in shorthand, and the proceedings closed to the public and press. There had never been an inquiry like it in Australian cycling circles. It took five full days and heard 25 witnesses.

The front bunch came under minute scrutiny. Corbett, Plunkett and O'Brien were examined in exhaustive detail for several hours each. Kett and Gordon, members of the bunch who dropped out early, were also asked a number of questions. But it didn't stop there. All other riders were called in for lengthy interviews.

Rumours abounded that the Council's inquiries were exceedingly broad. O'Brien said that 'I can assure you there will be some revelations at the inquiry which will startle the public'. He hinted at the breadth of charges when he said that 'If MacFarland had done his share of the pacing, the winner would have come from the back men'. One newspaper reported that it was 'understood' that there had been a large amount of betting on the part of some of the competitors and on the morning of the race 'even the gamins at the street corner were prophesying and advising those whom they loved to place their little bit of stuff on Corbett'.

For the promoters it cast a pall over the forthcoming Taylor–MacFarland match races. Then, on Friday, while the inquiry was still in full progress, Floyd MacFarland broke off the series of races with Taylor. He gave no reason, stating simply that he had good grounds for his action, and rebuffed all attempts at an interview. Within 48 hours of the starter firing his gun at The Sydney Thousand, the Australian cycling scene was in turmoil.

One week after The Sydney Thousand the Council of the New South Wales League of Wheelmen announced its decision. It was stunning. Of the 11 starters in the race, 7 were suspended from cycle racing. Floyd MacFarland got the longest suspension, three years. Larry Corbett, the winner, received a two-year suspension. The American, Hardy Downing, the New Zealander, Plunkett, and two Australians, Kett and Bathie, were each given a year's suspension. Gordon was given six months.

Alfred O'Brien was awarded the first prize of £750. With Corbett and Plunkett's names now crossed off, that left Major Taylor, the fourth place finisher, in second place and he was to be paid £100. Since the fifth place finisher, MacFarland, had also been disqualified, it was presumed that the sixth place finisher, Don Walker, would receive the third place prize of £50. Inexplicably, the Council ordered that money given to the League itself.

In an interview with *The Daily Telegraph* McIntosh explained the decision. He said that The Sydney Thousand was a 'fiasco' and in the interests of the sport 'drastic steps had to be taken'. He added that had O'Brien's appeal not been lodged it was the intention of the Council to hold an inquiry anyway. At that point McIntosh revealed the ethical stance of the League in relation to team riding.

The Federal Cycling Council:
1. Mr. Bolt (W.A.)
2. Mr J. Wright (Q)
3. Mr. H. D.
McIntosh (N.S.W.),
Vice-president 4. Mr.
Callaghan (VIC.),
President
5. Mr. Gazzard
(S.A.); 6. Mr. Gleeson
(VIC.), Secretary.

'The Council would not have minded so much if the front and back divisions had each taken one rider—it would have been one division against the other and would have made a good race as was the case last year—but when it was conclusively proved that two back markers worked in the interests of a man in the front bunch, then it was

138

time that the Council took severe measures'. McIntosh said that he had asked MacFarland, man-to-man, to 'make a good race' of it and MacFarland had told him that he would ride hard. He did not. McIntosh's message was that the Council had cleaned house.

The public did not think that the Council had cleaned house at all. McIntosh's statement that the Council had intended to inquire into the race anyway was thrown back in his face. He had been one of the stewards on the track who had dismissed O'Brien's initial protest. And why had Don Walker not received the third prize of £50? Not a breath of scandal had attached to him, he had not been suspended, and everyone agreed that during the race he had done more pacing than any other single person. The Council's response was that no 'official note' had been taken as to where he finished. Reports suggested that the inquiry cost the League £35 and the Council was effectively asking Walker to foot the bill.

Many could not understand why there was such a variety of penalties. There was a widespread feeling that 'a conspiracy is a conspiracy' and all the parties should be treated the same. The Council had explained that Gordon was leniently dealt with because he had suffered a severe fall last season. Many justifiably wondered what that had to do with the matter. It was suspected by many that MacFarland had been treated particularly harshly as punishment for having backed out of the Major Taylor match races at the last minute. *The Sydney Sportsman*'s view on that issue was unequivocal: 'The trail of the Summer Nights Amusement Syndicate is over the whole thing'. For MacFarland that must have been bitter irony. In early January, when he had received his disqualification for his clash with Taylor in the season's first race, the syndicate had brought its influence to bear in getting the penalty reduced to a £25 fine. MacFarland must have felt afterward that he was 'safe in anything he might do, and that the syndicate would see him through'. But a promoter as astute as McIntosh was capable of sensing the currents in the air and was undoubtedly piqued at the match race cancellation as well. Besides, the season was now over and Floyd was no longer needed.

Larry Corbett received some sympathy. In a dubious compliment *The Sydney Sportsman* contended that he was 'every bit as straight as most of the pedallers' and exceedingly generous and good natured. The sad thing was that given his talent and handicap he would have likely won a prize on his own merits if it had been a fair race. The lucky man, everyone agreed, was O'Brien. He was one of the distinctly lesser talents on the track and had made the final by being in easy heats. The amusing part was that 'those who were in on the alleged pool did not think him class enough to invite to have a share'.

By the time of the announcement most of the riders were in Seymour, Victoria preparing for the Australian Half Mile and One Mile Championships. It was in a hotel there that MacFarland and others first learned of the decision. Since it meant that the suspended riders could not participate in any further races anywhere in the world, Floyd and Hardy Downing returned immediately to Sydney to ask for a rehearing on the grounds that they were called as witnesses at an inquiry in which they did not even know that they were on trial. That defence received good support both within and without cycling circles. *The Australian Cyclist* thought that the New South Wales League of Wheelmen had adopted methods akin to a Star Chamber. As so many riders had so much to lose, the way the Council had dealt with it was just not good enough. While *The Referee* said that the Australian riders who had tied their fortunes to MacFarland 'got what they deserved', others felt that a man had the right to defend himself fairly in such circumstances.

The right to a fair defence did not imply sympathy, however. The public generally suspected that the three-year disqualification reflected sound proof that there was strong evidence against Mac-Farland. According to the Major, Floyd was no scapegoat. In his autobiography Taylor said that MacFarland had approached him three times to see if he would agree to combine with Floyd in the race. As the Major explained it, MacFarland knew that Taylor would not 'lay down' and lose, but Floyd could 'fix things' for Taylor to win, assuming he would split the purse. Taylor replied that he would not agree to anything that 'looked suspicious'. He would go so far as to share the pacing with MacFarland to catch the front bunch but at the finish 'may the best man win'. MacFarland refused the offer.

Even before the dust could clear, Larry Corbett, the dispossessed winner, conferred with solicitors about the legal power of the Council of the New South Wales League of Wheelmen to deprive him of the £750 first prize. Corbett felt that he had won it and he wanted it. He filed suit on May 6th. Twelve days later the Supreme Court of New South Wales ordered the disputed money to be handed over to the Court. For reasons not at all clear the court ordered O'Brien, rather than the syndicate or Council, to be defendant. It was now Corbett v. O'Brien, and a court would be making the decision. That would take nearly a year.

❖ ❖ ❖

Major Taylor's 1904 tour centred about Sydney, Melbourne and Adelaide, his time and activities controlled by the Sydney Summer Nights Amusement Committee and associated parties. However, his commitment was now over as per his original contract. But with Daisy expecting a child, they delayed the return journey to America until after the birth and he filled in time. Though his appearance fee, the prize money, ground rental, and associated administrative costs proved prohibitive to most would-be local promoters, the Major did pick up some whistle-stop money and sample the hospitality of small-town rural Australia.

In the New South Wales country town of Wagga Wagga the local cycling club arranged a 'Major Taylor Carnival'. It was a big day for the regional sheep growing centre, and among the cycling enthusiasts it was 'bustle and excitement. Some of them, it is feared, are off their meat'. *The Wagga Express* anticipated that every household in town and district for many miles around 'should be depleted of the majority if not all of their occupants', so they would be able to say that 'they were present at the great cycling meeting at which Major Taylor was the principle figure'.

Major Taylor arrived early on a Wednesday morning on the express train from Melbourne. He was driven directly to the Commercial Hotel where he chatted with officials. The 'popular little American' pleased them with his 'frank and easy manner and conversation'. In all likelihood he was the first black American members of that community would have seen. By three o'clock 1,800 people had arrived at the track; it was seldom in Wagga that one witnessed 'the almost complete circle of people around the course'. Taylor had his competitors 'at his mercy' in the first heat and the crowd 'did not forget to recognise it'. In the final he was so severely handicapped he never had a chance to catch the front men. The crowd was disappointed and an impromptu mile scratch race was put together on the spot, pitting the Major against his Adelaide ally, Bill MacDonald. Taylor beat him easily. After having contributed to the 'most successful event of its kind ever held in Wagga', the Major left that evening on the Sydney-bound train.

Taylor also made an appearance in Narrandera, New South Wales. Local sporting and business men had combined to guarantee Taylor's fee. Unfortunately, as a result of misunderstanding between local officials, no one met Taylor at the station platform that morning. He was consequently subjected 'to the infliction of attentions from Narrandera's public nuisance and a bevy of small boys'. Later that day some 800 people showed up at the Gillenbah track. As the *Narandera Argus* reported, the community anxiously awaited the Major's opinion. He said that it 'compared very favourably ... with most up-country tracks'. As in Wagga, Taylor was 'literally handicapped clean out of everything', so a special scratch mile race was subsequently subscribed on the spot. The Major 'did as he liked with the field'. He would allow them to gain a lead then sprint out ahead, then slow up till they caught up, then jump ahead again. The crowd loved it. At dinner that night in the Criterion Hotel they thanked him 'for doing his best to keep the sport clean'. The Narrandera Cycling Club had suffered a net loss of £5 on the meet, but the town was one of the few in Australia to see the living legend in action.

❖ ❖ ❖

Taylor also contracted to ride at a three-day meet in Adelaide, on the 9th 13th, and 16th of April. It was his favourite city and the scene of his greatest triumph during the tour. He thought it an ideal place to unwind. It proved otherwise.

In his first race, on the first day, a series of accusations and counter-accusations laced the air between the Major, officials, and other riders about failure to pace, and the arguments were renewed in every one of Taylor's rides over the next two race days. Two Australians were eventually fined. Unfortunately the officials agreed that Taylor was equally to blame but failed to fine him. The officials were subjected to great criticism in newspaper articles, editorials, and letters-to-the-editor for 'crawling to Taylor'. Great acrimony developed on all sides. On the last day Taylor rode only part of a single race, then quit. There was intense hostility on all sides.

In an interview published in *The Register* on April 18th, two days later, he said that 'I cannot exaggerate how sorry I am if the public have been disappointed. Without being egotistical, I think they were. Your people are generous in their enthusiasm, and they appreciate good, honest sport.' The Major had previously pointed out that there was no 'colour prejudice about the local spectators', but in the April 18th interview was vehement that 'some of your officials have all along entertained a disgusting prejudice against me'. Further, they 'have regarded me merely as a revenue earning machine; nothing more. My, I could fill your paper up with incidents of how this bias has been displayed. There are a few gentlemen in the league for whom I have the highest respect, and I believe I have had their support. But I guess I've had to contend with more on the other side'.

The journalist reporting the comments said that Taylor thumped him on the knee 'with almost painful emphasis and simultaneously stamped the floor with his feet. There was a suggestion of vigorous contempt in his demeanour'. For Taylor, the 1904 Australian cycling season had totally soured.

❖ ❖ ❖

On May 11th Daisy gave birth to a daughter, 'the first prize of our wedded life'. They christened her Rita Sydney in honour of the city that they so greatly admired. She was subsequently known to her friends as 'Sydney'. On June 6th, 1904, the family boarded an American-bound ship with a pet wallaby, some cockatoos and parrots, and the Australian champion, Don Walker. A large dockside crowd waved the Major off. He never returned.

❖ ❖ ❖

The great mystery of Taylor's second tour Down Under is: Exactly when did he learn that MacFarland and Lawson were also going to be in Australia? Did he know his nemesis would be there *before* he agreed to the tour terms and signed his contract? Would he have signed if he had known? And if he did know, was the money so great that even under such circumstances he was willing to accept the offer?

If, as Australian newspaper accounts indicate, MacFarland and Lawson were not paid any appearance fee by the syndicate, did the pair simply head south of their own accord? The immense amount of money on offer in Australia would certainly have been an attractive situation in and of itself. And once it was public knowledge that Taylor was going to be there again as well, it is easy to imagine MacFarland packing his bags.

However, given that concerns over the attendance and gate money were primary in the syndicate's thinking about the second tour, and that Tom Scott had specifically been sent to North America 'looking for cycling stars', a likely scenario is that the duo was actively sought out and invited down, even if not directly paid to come. A strong personal connection was in place since Lawson, now riding under MacFarland, had been in Australia two years before, had personally met McIntosh, and was known to the local cycling community. Given McIntosh's subsequent business, theatrical and sports promotion record and shrewdness, it seems likely that he would have assured that the pair was coming before committing so much money (£2,000, a third more than in 1903) to Taylor.

That begs another crucial question: If Hugh did know the pair was coming, and Taylor didn't, did McIntosh then keep the duo's visit secret from Taylor until he had signed him? Given the shadiness of many of McIntosh's business and personal dealings in his lifetime, it would have been absolutely in character for him to have done so. In support of that contention, McIntosh did not inform Taylor about the White Australia policy, either, before he came down on his first tour. As Taylor himself wrote, he only found out during the journey.

Was Taylor then, in effect, blindsided over the 1904 tour? There are some hints. Prior to Taylor's arrival there does not appear to have been any races scheduled other than the normal ones on the Sydney, Melbourne and Adelaide racing circuits, plus The Sydney Thousand. Newspaper accounts suggest that the series of match races arranged specifically between MacFarland, Lawson and Taylor in February were set up several weeks *after* Taylor arrived. And, as already noted, the promoters had to overcome stiff resistance from many Victorian League of Wheelmen members to even pull it off. Likewise the attempted scheduling of a five-race match between MacFarland and Taylor, to follow The Sydney Thousand, was another ad hoc post-arrival effort. So there appears to have been nothing in the initial season's scheduling that might have raised any alarm bells in Taylor's mind, or led him to suspect anything would be notably different about the 1904 tour.

So what did Taylor know, and when did he know it? In the conversation he had with *The Register* journalist in Adelaide, on April 18th, may be found a clue. At the end of the interview in which Taylor complained about the intense racism and ill treatment by South Australian League of Wheelmen officials, he added a final comment: 'On my journey over to Australia from America this time I felt almost impatient to get onto your track. The people gave me a splendid reception last year, and I was looking forward to my appearance with the keenest anticipation. And when I think of the result, well—I like the climate here, the track is easily the best in Australia, the people are great. But you must put your full stop there'. [In Australia the phrase 'full stop' is used to indicate the end of a sentence, or that a conversation is over.]

Would Taylor really have been 'almost impatient' had he know that MacFarland and Lawson would be in the country? Only definitive documentation—if such can ever be found—can confirm what Taylor knew, and when he knew it. But it is arguably the most intriguing unanswered question about his career.

Epilogue

THE END OF AN ERA

That was the 1904 cycling season in Australia. It proved to be the end of an era. Motor cycles and automobiles were already capturing the public imagination and those machines' greater speed was usurping the bicycle's claim to glory. Major Taylor, the premier international figure in the sport, predicted cycling's demise: 'When motor cars become affordable, cycles would be doomed'. Within a few years Americans, New Zealanders and Australians would be the top three users of motor vehicles in the world, per capita. The Sydney Cricket Ground's cycle track was removed in 1920, 24 years after the initial one was laid.

There were many cycling enthusiasts who had hoped that the importation of Major Taylor to Australia, with his high principles, would result in the cycling arena receiving not just an attendance boost, but 'much needed purification'. Unfortunately, after Taylor left the cycling waters were even murkier. As one writer commented, 'It used to be our proud boast that an athlete, no matter what his colour or nationality, could depend upon a fair field and no favour'. The other riders clearly did not give Taylor a fair deal in 1904. In an attempt at salvaging the Australian character, the writer added that 'Bad as we are, we are perhaps no worse than America (if that be any consolation)'.

After the Sydney Thousand scandal even *The Daily Telegraph*, the major publicity organ for the syndicate, editorialised on the issue of mixing mammon and men in sport-as-business.

> Sport is only valuable to the community in proportion to the manner in which it stimulates those instincts of healthy, chivalrous rivalry that make for manliness in the national character. When the public are given a display of track tricks and dodges for the selfish purpose of winning money prizes, it is not surprising if they eventually conclude that are being "humbugged" and eventually lose interest.

And they did. During his two Down Under tours Major Taylor had momentarily generated a massive resurgence in cycle racing's popularity. But when Floyd MacFarland and Iver Lawson returned to face Thorwald Elleggarde from Denmark and Walter Rutt of Germany in 1905 the interest was not nearly so intense, the news coverage not so extensive, nor the crowds anywhere near as large. Without the Major it wasn't the same.

THE WHITE AUSTRALIA POLICY

The White Australia Policy essentially remained in effect through WWII, but thereafter economic and political needs and pressures, and changes in sentiment, began to erode it. Asian students were allowed to study at Australian universities from 1950, through the Colombo Plan, and in 1958 the *Revised Migration Act* eliminated the dictation test. In 1973 the Whitlam government began dismantling White Australia policies and in 1975 the *Racial Discrimination Act* banned any use of racial criteria for official purposes. The country is now a highly desirable migrant destination. By 2006 one-sixth of the population spoke a language other than English at home, the most common being Italian, Greek, Arabic, Cantonese, Mandarin and Vietnamese.

The Bulletin

The Bulletin, launched in 1880 and Australia's longest-running magazine, was published for the last time in January, 2008. It had long ago dropped its 'White Australia' masthead.

THE SYDNEY THOUSAND

In the case of Corbett vs. O'Brien, proceedings were frequently delayed by Larry Corbett. He once claimed that he was unable to attend court since he had to work for six weeks in Western Australia. In a deposition O'Brien stated that the request was not bona fide as he had known the plaintiff 'for the last eight or nine years and during that period I have never known him to do any work'. It finally came to trial in March, 1905. Not surprisingly, in court a number of riders 'couldn't remember' various aspects of the arrangements made. At the outset the judge ruled that the *decision* reached by the Council of the League of Wheelmen (whether right or wrong) was not at issue in the courtroom, otherwise the legal system would be swamped by appeals from sportsmen. The matter before the jury was whether the Council had been *fair* in its inquiry. The jury decided 'yes' on all counts. Alfred O'Brien received the £750 first prize, but had to pay the syndicate's legal costs. In exchange, O'Brien's costs were to be paid by Corbett. Major Taylor was awarded the second prize of £100. No mention was made of third prize.

Larry Corbett's lawsuit had cost the syndicate and League Council much time and money during the course of the year-long matter. Interestingly, he was the only suspended cyclist to have to serve out his full (two-year) suspension. The Federal Cycling Council, of which McIntosh was soon to become vice-president, insisted there was no connection.

HUGH McINTOSH

Hugh McIntosh went on to other things, gripped by the notion that 'only big ideas produced big money'. And he had some big ones. Building upon his experience with the black cyclist, McIntosh promoted the first black–white world heavyweight championship boxing match, between Jack Johnson, the 'coloured champion of the world',

from Galveston, Texas, and Tommy Burns. Burns, a Canadian then-resident in America, but who spent much time in Australia, was seduced into breaking the colour line by an irresistible McIntosh offer: Tommy got £6,000, which he could keep, win or lose.

Several months prior to the fight McIntosh had completed construction of a wooden arena (known for decades as 'the Stadium') on leased land in Rushcutter's Bay. It opened on August 20, 1908 with a concert, and the first boxing match was held the next day. Four months later an estimated 26,000 spectators, paying

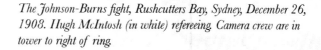

The Johnson-Burns fight, Rushcutters Bay, Sydney, December 26, 1908. Hugh McIntosh (in white) refereeing. Camera crew are in tower to right of ring.

from one shilling to £10 per seat, squeezed in to watch Johnson and Burns. Several hundred police and mounted officers were on hand to keep control as thousands were turned away (various accounts suggest it was in the tens of thousands), and many late arrivals with tickets never managed to get through at all and missed the fight. As it turned out, Burns had accepted his money under wise conditions, for on December 26, 1908, in Sydney, he was humiliated by Johnson. Hugh refereed. The gate takings were £26,200 and there were no scandals. But McIntosh had an even bigger and more farsighted

153

McIntosh in later life

idea. He scheduled it at 11:00 am, filmed it in the bright summer sunlight, and reportedly made a further £60,000 from Australian and overseas film rights.

Like many an entrepreneur McIntosh had his ups and downs. On the up side he became a very wealthy and influential man; bought controlling interest in *The Sunday Times* group; was a noted theatrical producer (the Tivoli Follies) who enjoyed the company of (and hired) many famous stars of the era; parked expensive cars outside expensive mansions, including leasing Lord Kitchener's former home in Kent, England; and held political office in New South Wales.

Jim Shepherd, author of *A History of Australian Speedway*, noted that no previously published work on McIntosh has ever mentioned his role in the development of early Australian motor racing. As a member of the New South Wales Parliament Hugh used his position to influence the New South Wales Lands Department to approve the building of the New-castle Speedway in 1925–1926; the Olympia Motor Speedway in southern Sydney's Maroubra suburb in 1925; and the following year the Sydney Showground's Speedway Royal—and may have been a silent partner in all three.

On the downside it all came apart, owing to profligate spending and poor management. In 1932 he suffered the finality of a spectacular slide into bankruptcy, owing large amounts of money to an equally large array of companies and individuals, including his own sister and close, long-term friends.

In a comeback effort he opened the Black and White Milk

Bar in London three years later, introducing that Australian concept to England. It was highly successful but quickly attracted imitators more astute and well-funded than he, and McIntosh's business collapsed. He died in England in January 1942, essentially penniless, at 65. His wife May died in 1959.

Don Walker

Don Walker left Australia with the Taylors for a holiday. The 'poisoning' of his mind was relatively short-lived and away from the intense pressure of the racially charged 1904 Australian season he resumed his close friendship with the Major. He tried his hand at a bit of overseas riding but was relatively unsuccessful. Walker's most intense memories of the land of the free were of the astonishing degree of racial vehemence that Taylor had to withstand there. Back in Australia Walker was long revered as one of the country's great cyclists. His 1898 Australian record of 29 seconds for the standing start quarter mile, unpaced, stood for 30 years. He finished his working life in Melbourne with Dunlop, the tyre and rubber manufacturer, and wore his trademark moustache to the end.

Iver Lawson

Iver Lawson left Australia after his disqualification. A few months later he won the world championship at the Crystal Palace in London. He returned to Australia in 1905 and 1906. Back in America in 1906 he suffered ptomaine poisoning and in a three-week fight for his life lost 35 pounds. His last trip to Australia in 1911 involved a series of six-day bicycle races. His sprinting abilities deteriorated with time and he finally gave the game away at the end of the 1915 season. Peter Nye reported that he saved virtually nothing from his career, apparently suffered from alcoholism as result of his brother's death in a cycling accident, and was last seen in 1948, dealing cards in Utah.

Hardy Downing

HARDY DOWNING

Hardy was an excellent cyclist who continued competing until 1914. After retirement he opened a gym in Salt Lake City and among his early clientele was the aspiring Jack Dempsey. Jack was always grateful and as Hardy lay dying in the hospital, in 1960, Jack visited him.

FLOYD MACFARLAND

By July 1904 MacFarland was asking for remission of his three-year suspension, or at least a fine in lieu. One Australian writer felt that MacFarland's appeal should be ignored, that his audacity was a 'preeminent trait in the mental composition of the sons of the stars and stripes'. In August the Council of the League of Wheelmen indicated that to show leniency by lessening the three-year penalty would 'be a fatal step for the sport and a very bad precedent'. The white Americans 'have proved themselves so utterly corrupt that their future presence would be a direct menace to the success of any meeting'. Yet, by whatever machinations, Floyd MacFarland was soon racing again. It seems that someone in Australia forgot to officially notify American and international cycling bodies of the sanctions—ever.

Floyd MacFarland returned to Australia for the 1905 season. His racing had its ups and downs, including a bad fall. In 1906 he returned yet again both to race and supervise the construction of a board track in Melbourne, which he also briefly managed. However, he was not pleased with various matters and vowed he would never again visit Australia. He kept his word.

Over the next several years MacFarland continued riding in his usual wide variety of events, from half-mile sprints to the incredibly gruelling six-day track races. However, by 1912 he turned his hand pretty much full time to race promotion and the management of tracks and riders, at which he had already proved himself a master. In the afternoon of April 17, 1915 MacFarland got into an argument with a concessionaire at the Newark Velodrome in New Jersey. Tempers quickly flared and Floyd was felled by a screwdriver blow behind his left ear. He died that night.

Floyd MacFarland's death clearly marked the end of another era. During the first quarter century of modern bicycle racing (1890–1915) Floyd had been in the thick of it all in more varied ways and more successfully than anyone else. He had ridden against, and personally beaten, most cyclists of note at one time or another, had managed numerous champions, and was the sport's premiere promoter when he died. Alf Goullet felt that the sport was never managed as well afterward. Floyd MacFarland's funeral was attended by 1,500 and The New York Times devoted two columns and a photograph to him.

Australia does owe Floyd MacFarland a debt, however. He was instrumental in spotting and bringing to America several of Aus-

Floyd MacFarland (standing) with Jackie Clark

tralia's cycling talents and developing them into some of the best in the world. There is no question that the outstanding international reputations earned early in the 20th century by such Australian riders as Alf Grenda, Jackie Clark, Ernie Pye and the legendary Alf Goullet were due in great part to his managerial and promotional astuteness.

Today Australia, a country of just over 22 million people, is among the world's cycle-racing powerhouses. Between January and March, 2010, for example, Australia as a nation sat atop the Union Cycliste Internationale world rankings; Australian women held number one ranking in three of the eight Women's Elite track racing categories; Australian men sat atop three of the four Mountain Bike categories; and in BMX an Australian was the overall top ranked male rider, while Australians held three of the top eight women's positions.

MAJOR TAYLOR

The pair of Australian tours was etched indelibly on Major Taylor's memory. The 1904 Australian season had been 'the most strenuous as well as the most eventful period' of his professional life. It was a striking contrast to the 1903 season, which was the most enjoyable he ever experienced. Although the two trips represented less than 5 per cent of his entire professional cycle racing career, he devoted 35 per cent of his 431-page autobiography to them.

When Major Taylor left Australia he returned to his home in Massachusetts with his wife and new daughter. There, as he described it, he 'suffered a collapse and narrowly averted a nervous breakdown'. He attributed it to his 'strenuous campaign in Australia augmented by the incidental worries of life'. He did not race again for three years. During that time his incidental worries were added to by a $10,000 law suit filed by Continental promoters for breach of contract through failing to show in Europe in the 1904 season. It dragged through court and was eventually settled when the Major agreed to ride in Europe again, both to end the suit and for the money. The relentless pressure was put upon the Major because he was needed overseas. As in Australia and America, European cycle racing was declining as a mass spectator sport.

During the three-year lay-off the Major gained 30 pounds.

He worked hard to get back to his racing trim of 168 pounds and when he did proved to be the Major Taylor of old. On the 1907 tour he defeated many veterans and a number of rising stars. To put to rest any doubts about his talents and abilities he broke two world records on the Paris Buffalo track. By the time he left the Continent he had won 32 first places. Victor Breyer, the Continental promoter, considered Major Taylor 'the savior of cycling in Europe, the greatest racer and drawing card of them all'. That was no small praise.

Taylor raced in Europe for two more seasons, during which he sacrificed a fundamental principle and agreed to ride on Sundays, and then decided to wrap it up abroad. In 1910 he had a final shot at America. In Salt Lake City, in August, he raced against some of his old Australian nemeses, including Hardy Downing and Iver Lawson, but fared poorly.

When he retired that year, at the age of 32, he had spent half his life pedalling bicycles around the tracks of the world. The remarkable career had taken its toll, most notably through 'the great mental strain and the utter exhaustion' brought about by that 'monster prejudice, both on and off the track. In most of my races I not only struggled for victory, but also for my very life and limb'.

That was not self-serving hyperbole. Upon Taylor's retirement the editor of the Sydney Referee wrote that in his opinion the Major was

> the greatest racing cyclist the world has ever seen and his wonderful record was gained under very often the most adverse conditions; for he was hustled and hated as only a coloured person can be by the superior men in God's country, and he did not always receive fair play on the Continent or even here in Australia. Had he not been a marvel of pluck, speed and skill, he would have either been killed outright or disabled years ago. Cycle racing is a very dangerous game, even under ordinary conditions, but when deliberate fouling is introduced, it is then too risky

for even the most daring. Yet Major Taylor often had to chance it. Like all other mortals, he had his failings, but he was one of the straightest athletes that ever entered the arena.

Major Taylor's swan song was on September 16, 1917, at the Newark Velodrome, at an old-timers race. Birdie Munger, his early mentor, held him for the start of what the *Newark Evening News* called 'The Rheumatic Stakes Feature'. The Major beat the other ten riders.

Taylor's later life was tragic. After retirement he suffered serious medical and financial problems. Investments went bad and eventually he had to sell his large house—his private refuge for 25 years. In 1930 his 28-year marriage ended. He spent his last two years essentially destitute, peddling copies of his book on the south side of Chicago, living in a YMCA. He died on June 21, 1932, in the charity ward of the Cook County Hospital. He was survived by his estranged wife and daughter, Sydney, whom he had not seen in seven years.

Major Taylor, at one time the world's highest paid athlete in the world's most popular sport, and in several countries the most widely watched black athlete for decades, had only one obituary published, in the *Chicago Defender*, a black newspaper. *The American Bicyclist* made only brief reference to him and, as Andrew Ritchie pointed out, his death was not even mentioned in newspapers in New York City. Thus passed one of the United States' truly great sports figures. America was not kind to his memory.

Taylor's wife, Daisy, died in April, 1965, at the age of 89. His daughter Sydney, the last direct connection to Australia, died in 2005, aged 101.

❖ ❖ ❖

Taylor's resurrection began in a small way in 1948, when Frank Schwinn, the American bicycle magnate, financed the exhumation and reburial of Major Taylor's body and the erection of a memo

Taylor's wife, Daisy, died in April, 1965, at the age of 89. His daughter Sydney, the last direct connection to Australia, died in 2005, aged 101

rial headstone at the Mount Glenwood Memory Gardens in Illinois. In 1982 the Major Taylor Velodrome in Indianapolis, Indiana was dedicated; Taylor's daughter attended. A Major Taylor Association was formed in Worcester, Massachusetts in 1998, and a monument to Major Taylor, a two-sided sculpture wall, was unveiled at the Worcester Public Library on May 21, 2008. Today, numerous pedallers ride together under the banner of one or another of the more than two dozen Major Taylor cycling clubs found around the country.

Acknowledgements and Sources

I am grateful to Paul Barron, of Barron Films (Perth and Toronto), for taking a few moments to glance over my submission to his studio, in mid-1987, appreciating Taylor's significance (though Paul had never heard of him), and deciding that it would make an interesting movie. It was the only unsolicited, over-the-transom project he had ever taken on. It forced me to finally sit down and write my book manuscript for him to work from. It premiered as a two-hour movie, *Tracks of Glory*, on the Disney Channel in 1992, and the four-hour version won the 1993 Logie Award (Australia's 'Emmy') as the 'Most Popular Telemovie or Mini-series'.

I would especially like to thank Maureen Lyus for typing the original manuscript from my taped dictation, under great pressure (it was written in 28 days). She was marvellous. Being paid by the hour, she also became progressively cheaper during my descriptions of the racing when, as she confided, she found herself typing faster and faster to find out what happened to the Major.

I wish to thank those who have taken the time to read the manuscript: Richard Crepeau, Professor of History at the University of Central Florida, and former President of the North American Society for Sports History; Mel Davies, Honorary Research Fellow in Economic History at the University of Western Australia, and former Commonwealth and international cyclist of note; Philip Derriman, Sydney Cricket Ground historian; Karen Brown Donovan, Major Taylor's great grand-daughter and keeper of the flame; Michael McKernan, formerly of the University of New South Wales, and a leading light in Australian sports history studies; Peter Nye, author of numerous cycling histories and a doyen of the genre; Andrew Ritchie, prolific cycling historian and Taylor's biographer; Jim Shepherd, historian and member of the Sydney Cricket Ground Museum Task Force; Ronald A. Smith, Emeritus Professor of Exercise and Sport Science at the Pennsylvania State University, and Secretary-Treasurer of the North American Society for Sports History for some 30 years; Frank Van Straten, Hugh McIntosh's biographer; and Bernard Whimpress, former Curator of the Adelaide Oval Museum and Historian of the South Australian Cricket Association. Their comments, insights and corrections were invaluable and are deeply appreciated. Any errors are my responsibility.

A special thanks is in order to the all the staff at various libraries in Australia and New Zealand who have helped in obtaining articles, photos and leads to information about Major Taylor, and to innumerable individuals who have taken an interest in the topic and offered thoughts over the years. Most research work was completed between 1976 and 1982, so a number of them have passed away. However, to those still alive, and to those who have helped in the final preparation, I want you to know that it would not have happened otherwise.

Roberta Blake edited the final manuscript and my wife, Roey was the ever-willing—and most severe—critic. When the manuscript was finished, she designed the book.

SOURCES

The foundation for this book was provided by the numerous Australian newspapers, magazines and journals that wrote about Major Taylor. Some gave extensive coverage and produced lengthy articles, while others provided only a passing glimpse. Collectively, they enable a strong sense of the national mood and reaction to the Major to be pulled together. The ones I found particularly valuable were *The Advertiser* (Adelaide); *The Argus* (Melbourne); *The Arrow* (Sydney); *The Bulletin* (Sydney); *The Canterbury Times* (Christchurch); *The Daily Telegraph* (Sydney); *The Herald* (Melbourne); The *Kalgoorlie Miner*; *The Narandera Argus* (it is spelled correctly, for those Australians who know it as Narrandera today); The *Narandera Ensign*; *The Newcastle Herald*; *The Observer* (Adelaide); *The Register* (Adelaide); *The Sunday Times* (Sydney); *The Sydney Mail*; *The Sydney Morning Herald*; *The Sydney Sportsman*; *The Star* (Sydney); *The Town & Country Journal* (Sydney); *The Truth* (Melbourne); *The Wagga Advertiser*; *The Wagga Wagga Express*; *The Weekly Press* (New Zealand); and *The Worker* (Brisbane and Sydney versions).

Another important element in researching Major Taylor's Australian tours was his autobiography, which devoted 150 of its 431 pages to the Australian period alone. It was titled *The Fastest Bicycle Rider in the World: The Story of a Colored Boy's Indomitable Courage and Success Against Great Odds*, and was published by the Wormley Publishing Company, in Worcester, Massachusetts in 1928. It is important for two reasons. For one thing, about 80 per cent of it consists of newspaper clippings, which provide a superb set of varied sources. Unfortunately, the Major rarely identified which newspaper he was quoting or reproducing, and in trying to piece together the racial and social background and sentiments, it is critical. *The Daily Telegraph*, which the Major drew heavily upon in Australia, was an important publicity organ for the Sydney Summer Nights Amusement Committee and has to be taken with a grain of salt. *The Bulletin*, which was not used by Taylor, was generally cynical and must also be taken in carefully measured doses. However, it provided a superb antidote to *The Daily Telegraph*, and in its parodies of the craze over the Major conveys some elemental truths in a way no other publication does. Others, such as *The Worker* (both the Brisbane and Sydney versions) swung wildly from adulation to relatively objective comments to seemingly unfounded criticism.

The other principal importance of the Major's autobiography is that it offers his view of matters, albeit written a quarter century later. Some facts are inaccurate, not unexpected after such a time, and he appears to have constructed dialogues between himself and others to make a point. Also, being so much reportage, it is often stilted to read and has many gaps, but the autobiography gives an insight not otherwise available.

The late Sir Hubert Opperman lent me his personal copy of Major Taylor's book and talked to me about him. As one of the world's cycling greats in the 1920s and 1930s Sir Hubert associated with a number of riders who knew, and had ridden against, the Major and was able to provide me with some valuable observations and comments.

A detailed analysis of the impact of the bicycle upon Australia is provided in my book *The Bicycle and the Bush: A Study of Man and Machine in Rural Australia* (Melbourne: Oxford University Press), 1980. Although it focuses upon the extensive use of the cycle in the rural environment, it provides an overall picture of the 'pushbike's' influence upon the 1890s urban scene as well. Among the few contemporary books surveying the general cycling scene in Australia near the turn of the century were F.G.C.Hanslowe's single issue of the *Australian Cycling Annual* (1897); Leonard Henslowe's *Cycling: The Sport and Pastime* (1897); and E. Lincoln's *New South Wales Motorists' and Cyclists' Annual 1905. The Australian Encyclopaedia* allowed me to prepare a relatively long and detailed entry (as encyclopaedias go) on 'Cycling', and also included an entry by Ray Martin and myself on 'Cycle Racing'.

The Australian cycle racing scene in bicycling's heyday, prior to Major Taylor's visit, is outlined in my chapter 'The Spectrum of Australian Bicycle Racing: 1890-1900', in Richard Cashman and Michael McKernan (eds.), *Sport in History* (St. Lucia, Qld.: University of Queensland Press), 1979. Keith Dunstan's chapter, 'The Pedalling Passion', in his book *Sports* (Melbourne: Sun Books), 1981, looks at selected aspects of cycle racing at the turn of the century. Gordon Inglis' *Sport and Pastime in Australia*, 1912, includes a brief chapter on cycle racing. H. 'Curly' Grivell's *Australian Cycling in the Golden Days* (Adelaide: privately published), 1951, is a collection of biographical sketches not only of early Australian racing cyclists but notable overseas visitors, including Major Taylor, Floyd MacFarland, and Iver Lawson. He is relatively patchy, however, in covering their careers. Bernard Whimpress's recent booklet, *'Major' Taylor at Adelaide Oval*, (Kent Town: privately published), 2005, is from the perspective of the former Curator of the Oval Museum and draws upon various newspaper coverage and Museum materials.

There were a number of Australian cycling journals in the 1890s but the only one national in scope, and that lasted until the Major's visit, was *The Australian Cyclist*, later to become the *Australian Cyclist and Motor-Car World*. It had excellent descriptions of Taylor's two tours, and his Melbourne races in particular.

Background material on Hugh McIntosh was obtained initially from Chris Cunneen's entry in *The Australian Dictionary of Biography*, Vol. 10, 1891-1939 (Melbourne: Melbourne University Press), 1986; and from Richard Broome's article on 'The Australian Reaction to Jack Johnson, Black Pugilist, 1907-9', in Cashman and McKernan's book *Sport in History*, cited earlier. However, these are upstaged by Frank Van Straten's *Huge Deal: The Fortunes and Follies of Hugh D. McIntosh* (South Melbourne: Thomas C. Lothian), 2004, the first full biography on him. It is an excellent work about a remarkable character and was far too long in coming. In personal correspondence and discussion, Jim Shepherd, author of *A History of Australian Speedway*, provided the information about McIntosh's hitherto never-mentioned role in Australian motor racing. He also noted that most visiting overseas and interstate cyclists apparently were housed at the Olympic Hotel, on Moore Park Road.

In America, Major Taylor was only briefly referred to in various sports histories prior to 1988. Examples are George Gipe's *The Great American Sports Book* (New York: Doubleday), 1978; Edwin B. Henderson and the editors of *Sport* magazine, *The Black Athlete: Emergence and Arrival* (New York: Publishers Company Inc.), 1978; John A. Lucas and Ronald A. Smith, *Saga of American Sport* (Philadelphia: Lea & Febiger), 1978; and Benjamin G. Rader's *American Sports: From the Age of Folk Games to the Age of Spectators* (Englewood Cliffs, N J: Prentice-Hall), 1983. Richard Mandell, in the April 12, 1971, issue of *Sports Illustrated*, gave a two-page summary of Taylor's career, in 'The Major Made It on a Bike'. All of those, however, tended to tease rather than satisfy one's curiosity to know more about him.

The turning point in the study of Taylor was 1988. Andrew Ritchie's book, *Major Taylor: The Extraordinary Career of a Champion Bicycle Racer* (San Francisco: Bicycle Books, Inc.) came out that year, the first full biography on the Major (revised in 2009). It is the basic starting point for future research on him. Also that year, Arthur Ashe, Jr. produced his comprehensive and ambitious work, *A Hard Road to Glory: A History of the African-American Athlete 1619-1918* (New York: Warner Books), in which he devoted four pages to Major Taylor. Peter Nye's *Hearts of Lions: The History of American Bicycle Racing* (New York: W.W.Norton & Company) was published in 1989 but was actually completed in 1987. It is a highly readable historical survey of the history of American bicycle racing and devotes the better part of 20 pages to Major Taylor. Importantly, it also includes substantial material on Floyd MacFarland, including his non-racing roles as manager and promoter, which I drew upon. The works of Ashe, Nye and Ritchie are fundamental to introducing Taylor in a way, and on a scale, not previously done in America; for that they must be thanked. It was an introduction long overdue.

None of those three works nor others that have followed present much information about Major Taylor's Australian tours. In particular one does not gain from them an appreciation or sense of how critical the second Australian tour was in the Major's career. The fact that he spent 35 per cent of his autobiography covering the Australian period underscores its significance to him.

The two-hour telemovie version of *Tracks of Glory* has been re-run on various US cable channels over the years, bringing Taylor's name and Australian experience to the attention of present day television viewing audiences. Notwithstanding the artistic liberties that were necessarily taken to convert it into a screenplay, the Australian screenwriter, Tony Morphett, accurately focused upon the basic issues and problems that Taylor had to contend with in his career. In association with the premiere of the telemovie, Peter Nye wrote a cover story on Major Taylor for the *USA Today*'s sports section (May 13, 1992), interviewing me about Taylor's Australian period and the creation of the film. Unfortunately the film has not been available for rental or purchase in America. At the time of writing, another film is planned, based upon Ritchie's research into Taylor's overall career (see *majorthemovie.com*).

A NOTE ON TAYLOR'S EARNINGS

When I first ran across reference to Major Taylor I was researching intently into 1900 Australia, so had a sense of what a pound would buy at that time. I was amazed to read how much he was winning in one race, or over the course of a three-day meet. When preparing the introduction to this book I wanted the present day reader to grasp what a £100 purse for a single race, a £1,500 appearance fee, or his total season's take represented. Given that Taylor's 1903 tour earned him 22 times as much as the average Australian worker made that year, I thought it would be particularly instructive to stack that up against present day athletes' and workers' relative incomes. It just so happened that Tiger Woods was in Australia the month I was revising. As he, like Taylor in his day, was the world's highest paid athlete and had received a highly publicised appearance fee to come to Australia, it was a particularly apt, timely and interesting comparison. The results offered a new perspective on the scale of money revolving around Taylor.

Information on average Australian wage earnings circa 1903–1904 was drawn from various state *Statistical Registers* of the time. The 'award wage' at the time (which is similar to a 'minimum wage' today) was £120 per year—enough to basically live on. However, as economic historian Mel Davies suggested, the figure of £182 per year, which was the wage of a bank teller or carpenter at the time, is probably more representative of an 'average' Australian's income, and has been used. So Taylor earned 22 times the average Australian's income (£4,000/£182). In November, 2009 the average Australian's full-time adult ordinary [non-overtime] earnings was AU$1,223 per week, or AU$63,600 annually (Australian Bureau of Statistics 6302.0, 'Average Weekly Earnings, Australia, Nov 2009'). Thus, Taylor's 1903 £4,000 income—22 times an average worker's wages—would equate to AU$1,400,000 today, the same value as the US$ in December 2010. Exchange rates can and do vary, of course, sometimes quickly and substantially. Notwithstanding that, for the present day Australian and American reader the bottom line is quite clear—the magnitude of Taylor's earnings is remarkable.

In discussions with Ron Smith I obtained general background information and some valuable thoughts on the range of earnings among various American professional sportsmen during Taylor's time. American professional baseball players' earnings, and how they compared with labourers' wages at the turn of the century, came from Harold Seymour's *Baseball: The Golden Age* (New York: Oxford University Press), 1971. I set the average American labourer's earnings at the time at $600, within the range offered by Seymour.

The Australian pound in Taylor's day was tied to the British pound, which was worth US$4.88 in early 1904, according to exchange rates published in the *Wall Street Journal*. Rounding it to five dollars makes calculations simple: a £100 pound prize was worth $500 American dollars (with an error of 2.4 per cent) at the time.

Taylor's 1903 Australian appearance fee of £1,500 was mentioned a number of times in Australian periodicals, interviews, and so on, his income being a major topic. As noted previously in this work, his earnings and that of other riders in 1903 year were specifically tallied by an Australian journalist at the end of the season, and Taylor's was cited as £4,000. In considering the appearance fee, number of wins and placings, the purses, and their value, it appears accurate, if rounded. His reported earnings of an additional £6000 during his 1903 summer European tour was cited later in Australian newspapers. That would have made his total take for the year £10,000. That was 55 times the average Australian's wages at the time, or in current day equivalent earnings, $3,500,000.

For the 1904 tour, in no source I read did anyone offer an end-of-the-year figure for total earnings by the riders. The impression is that the intense rivalry and racing overshadowed interest in the earnings. Furthermore, since The Sydney Thousand winner was not decided until a year later, any figures would have been grossly incomplete without it. Certainly Taylor, MacFarland and Lawson all had substantial success on the track. However, MacFarland and Lawson shared their money around (though how much and in what proportion is not known). Given that fact, and Taylor's £2,000 tour fee, he presumably would have taken home more money than anyone else.

I say presumably, because given the penchant for MacFarland and Lawson to engage in 'arrangements', and the opportunities which that afforded for off-track betting, they could have taken home a lot. As noted in the text, when Lawson was preparing to leave for overseas, he specifically commented to a reporter that he was 'more than pleased' with the financial results that year.

As to how much Taylor won over his lifetime, I wouldn't venture a guess. Many figures have been thrown around, whether for a given year, or tour, or how much potential income was lost through not riding on Sundays. But no one, to my knowledge, has attempted a career estimate. It would seem an interesting exercise for someone to pin down, given the increasing interest in his groundbreaking efforts, and his phenomenal earnings, in early American professional sports.

ILLUSTRATIONS

The illustrations are drawn mostly from Australian sources contemporaneous with Taylor's visits, in particular, newspapers, weekly magazines, and cycling journals. The original sources are unknown for three photographs of Taylor, one of Hugh McIntosh in later life, and several of circa 1900 Australian urban scenes; they are indicated as from the 'Author's Collection'. In any case, photographs taken in Australia prior to 1955 are in the public domain.

Some original illustration sources were fragile and copied manually many years ago, prior to the digitisation of collections. I am grateful to the staff members at the Battye Library, Perth, Western Australia; the Christchurch City Library, New Zealand; the La Trobe Library Collection, State Library of Victoria, Melbourne; the Mitchell Library, State Library of New South Wales, Sydney; the National Library of Australia, Canberra; the State Library of South Australia, Adelaide; and *The Observer* newspaper (Adelaide), for considerable help in obtaining usable reproductions. A particular debt is owed to my wife, Roey, for her extremely patient efforts with Photoshop to bring several back to life. For providing specific illustrations, I wish to thank Bernard Hempseed in New Zealand; and in America, Peter Nye, Board member of the United States Bicycling Hall of Fame, and Andrew Ritchie.

AN EXTRAORDINARY ATHLETE

iv. Marshall W. Taylor, *The Fastest Bicycle Rider in the World*, copy courtesy of Andrew Ritchie.

PRELUDE TO AUSTRALIA

x. White Australia [music]: march of the great white policy, composed by W. E. Naunton, 1910, National Library of Australia, nla. mus-vn3118296.

CHAPTER 1: TAYLOR IS IN TOWN

2. Author's collection.

4-5. Author's collection.

6. Author's collection.

7. *The Bulletin*, 17 January, 1903, p. 19.

8. *The Town & Country Journal*, 30 December, 1908, p. 28.

10. NSW State Library, Home and Away, hall_34775.

14. *The Bulletin*, 17 January, 1903. p. 19.

15. *The Town & Country Journal*, 7 January, 1903, p. 38.

17. *The Town & Country Journal*, 7 January, 1903, p.38.

18. *The Town and Country Journal*, 7 January 1903, p. 38.

CHAPTER 2: THE WORCESTER WHIRLWIND

20. *The Daily Telegraph*, 5 January 1903, p. 6.

23. *The Town and Country Journal*, 7 January 1903, p. 38.

26-27. *The Town and Country Journal*, 14 January 1903, p. 38.

28. Major and Mrs Taylor in Adelaide, Adelaide *Chronicle*, 4 April 1904, p. 44.

30-31. La Trobe Collection, State Library of Victoria, CB5/6/14/6.

33. Author's collection. This photograph has been identified on at least one American cycling website as taken at the Sydney Cricket Ground, and copyright invalidly claimed. However, Bernard Whimpress, former Curator of the Adelaide Oval Museum and Historian of the South Australian Cricket Association, says the background fence and railing details (on the larger, uncropped image) place it at the Adelaide oval. The original publication source is unknown.

34-35. Adelaide *Observer*, 4 April 1903, p. 597.

CHAPTER 3: THE FRINGES OF HONESTY

36. *The Bulletin*, 12 March 1898.

39. Courtesy State Library of Western Australia, The Battye Library, 000727D.

43. *The Sydney Mail*, 11 March, 1903, p. 603.

46. *The Town and Country Journal*, 11 March, 1903, p. 22.

CHAPTER 4: DOWN UNDER AGAIN

52. The Christchurch City Library, CCL PhotoCD 4, IMG0080.

55. Christchurch City Library File Reference: CCL PhotoCD 1, IMG0044.

56. *The Weekly Press* (New Zealand), 30 December 1903, p. 37.

58. Courtesy Bernard Hempseed.

CHAPTER 5: MACFARLAND AND LAWSON

58. Courtesy State Library of Western Australia, The Battye Library, 5501B/1.

61. Adelaide *Observer*, 13 February 1904, p. 26.

62. Adelaide *Observer*, 6 February 1904, p. 24.

63. Courtesy State Library of Western Australia, The Battye Library, 5501B/2.

64-65. Courtesy State Library of Western Australia, The Battye Library, 5501B/3.

Chapter 6: A Chill in the Air

66. *The Bulletin*, 1902, 1910, any issue.

Chapter 7: Rough Tactics

74. *The Weekly Times*, 31 January, 1903, p. 11.

76. Various.

79. Various.

Chapter 8: Melbourne: The Battle of the Champions

82. Author's collection.

84-85. Adelaide *Observer*, 17 January, 1903, p. 26.

86-87. *The Australasian*, 12 December 1896, p. 1170.

88. Various.

Chapter 9: Taylor Vs. Macfarland

90. *The Argus*, 13th February, 1904.

94-95. *The Australasian*, 30 January 1897, p. 227.

Chapter 10: The Incident

100. *The Argus*, 16th February, 1904.

102-103. *The Australasian*, 30 January 1897, p. 227.

105. *The Australian Cyclist and Motor-car World*, 25 February, 1904.

106. Courtesy of Richmond [Victoria] Local History Photograph Collection.

Chapter 11: Inquiry and Aftermath

108. *The Australian Cyclist and Motor-Car World*, February 25, 1904.

111. Author's Collection.

114. Image courtesy of the State Library of South Australia. SLSA: B 3787 - George Ruthven Le Hunte, ca. 1900.

Chapter 12: The Adelaide Episode

116. Adelaide *Observer*, 13 Feb 1904, p. 1.

118. Adelaide *Chronicle*, 27 February 1904, p. 44.

119. *The Town and Country Journal*, 11 March 1903, p. 22.

120-121 Adelaide *Chronicle*, 23 January 1904, pp. 199-199.

121. Taylor (arrowed), trapped in a pocket, unknown source.

122. Adelaide *Chronicle*, 27 Feb 1904, p. 44.

123. Adelaide *Chronicle*, 27 Feb, 1904, p. 464.

124. Adelaide *Chronicle*, 27 February 1904, p. 464.

CHAPTER 13: THE SYDNEY THOUSAND

126. NSW State Library DL PX 136, a1972006.

128. *The Sydney Mail*, 18 March 1903, p. 236.

131. NSW State Library DL PX 136, a1972002.

CHAPTER 14: THE STORM

132. *The Sydney Sportsman*, 6th April, 1904.

136. *The Referee*, 7 June 1905, p. 1

EPILOGUE

148-149. Burns-Johnson boxing contest, December 26th 1908, photographed by Charles Kerry, National Library of Australia Picture Collection, vn3060336-V

150. Author's Collection.

151. United States Bicycling Hall of Fame.

154. United States Bicycling Hall of Fame.

157. Courtesy of Andrew Ritchie.

A PERSONAL NOTE

I first ran across reference to Major Taylor in 1976, when researching the use of the bicycle in the Australian outback. Australian newspaper accounts in 1902–1904 referred to a world-famous, visiting black American cyclist with amazing talents and astounding earnings. I became more than curious. I was incredulous. Although I have lived in Australia for 25 years, I grew up in America. I knew of, and had read about, ground-breaking black athletes such as Jackie Robinson, Jessie Owens, and Jack Johnson. I had never even *heard* of Major Taylor.

I began keeping notes on him. In 1982 I returned to the topic for a brief period of intense research, then filed it all away. In mid-1987 I brought the story of Taylor's Australian tours to the attention of Paul Barron. After writing the book manuscript for his screenwriter to work from, I headed back to America. While passing through Sydney I mentioned to publisher Warren Salomon, for whom I had contributed numerous articles in *Bicycling Australia*, what I had just written. He recalled that he had been contacted some years before by someone in the United States doing research on Taylor. He thought it was Andrew Ritchie. When I returned to America I finally ran down Andrew's telephone number through his publisher.

I will never forget the conversation. From Orlando, I reached Ritchie in the San Francisco Bay area. I introduced myself and informed him that I had just completed a book on Major Taylor's Australian experiences. To the extent that emotion can be transmitted over the telephone, I sensed that Andrew was stunned. He said nothing for a *long* time, then informed me that earlier *that very day*, he had submitted to his publisher the final pages of *his* manuscript on Taylor's life. It was my turn to be stunned. An Englishman in America and an American in Australia had each, independently, 'discovered' Major Taylor and had conceived, researched and written books on him over the same period.

Andrew, unfortunately, never got to Australia—both time and money had been in short supply. Consequently I sent him, express, the next day, a copy of my manuscript to read. He made a few changes to his work, especially in his chapter on the Australian tours, and returned my manuscript with some comments and corrections of fact. When his book came out, the first biography on Taylor—and still the gold standard—I drew upon it for a dozen sentences about the end of Taylor's life. Other than those minor exchanges, the two books remain independent, and complementary.

Ritchie's book sweeps across the Major's life, devoting only five pages to the Australian tours. Mine focuses entirely upon the pressures and circumstances of the Down Under periods. As Andrew wrote to me, 'I think the thing I am left with most powerfully from reading your account of the two Australian years, is why MT was so utterly exhausted and ready to quit cycling by June, 1904. What a mess the whole thing was!'

When I finally received a copy of Andrew's book (I had not had the opportunity to see a manuscript), I immediately turned to the last two chapters. I had written on the Major in his heyday, at the peak of his fame, feted by Australia's Lord Mayors, and staying at the most prestigious hotels. I mentally lived with his Australian experiences for years, knowing of him only as an Australian celebrity, and nothing of his later personal circumstances. When I finished reading Andrew's account of the end of Taylor's life and his unclaimed body, I sat for a long, long while, deeply saddened that such a great human being and athlete, someone so famous in Europe, America and the Antipodes, could have been so quickly and so thoroughly forgotten.

Index

About the Author

Jim Fitzpatrick was born in Elkton, Maryland and grew up in southern California, where he graduated from UCLA. After serving with the Peace Corps in El Salvador, he moved to Australia, where he has spent most of his adult life and professional career. He earned a PhD in Human Sciences at The Australian National University.

He has been Director of Major Gifts for the Salvation Army in Phoenix, Arizona; Executive Administrator of the Australian Spinal Research Foundation; Project Director for a National Library of Australia Oral History Project; Research Officer with the Education Department of Western Australia; an urban planner in southern California; and has taught in the Geography Departments of the Universities of Natal, Western Australia, and New England.

He is the author of several books and numerous articles and reports on health, education, urban planning, cycling and history.

The Australian Logie Award-winning film, 'Tracks of Glory', was based on this book.

www.starhillstudio.com.au

The Bicycle in Wartime (Revised Edition) by Jim Fitzpatrick

The Bicycle in Wartime is a landmark work in the field of military history. Complemented throughout with an extensive collection of archival photographs, maps and early book, newspaper and magazine illustrations, this new edition has been revised to include new text and photographs and additional material on 21st century military cycle technology.

Reviews of the first edition:

Impressive breadth and detailed coverage of the use of bicycles in war. Jim Fitzpatrick shows convincingly how often experts were totally wrong in underestimating the influence of the bicycle even when used against highly mechanized armies. A fascinating and rewarding book to read.
—David Gordon Wilson, Emeritus Professor of Engineering at MIT, author of *Bicycling Science*

In this memorable tour de force, author Jim Fitzpatrick has, for the first time, traced the history of the bicycle in wartime. His contribution is significant and will stand the test of time ... the world's military forces have long been aware of [the bicycle's] potential. On occasion it has spelled the difference tetween victory and defeat: the Japanese in Malaya, the Viet Minh forces of Gen. Vo Nguyen Giap at Dien Bien Phu.
—Cecil B. Currey, author of *Victory at Any Cost: The Genius of Vietnam's General Vo Nguyen Giap*

An intriguing and compelling read, complemented by a multitude of archive photographs. Most important, the book brings together the strategic side of military policy and the experiences of cyclists on the ground.
—Paul Rosen, University of York

The Bicycle in Wartime is fascinating and important. In war [the bicycle] has kept surprising us. This is a stimulating and entertaining book. The illustrations are splendid. I can't imagine anyone who wouldn't enjoy reading it.
—Len Deighton, author of *Blitzkrieg*

The Bicycle and the Bush by Jim Fitzpatrick

The Bicycle and the Bush, cited in the Judges' Report of the 1981 Australian National Book Council Awards, is a superbly illustrated study of the widespread use of the bicycle in the vast Australian Outback by rural workers from 1890 into the 20th century. The machine was a mainstay for Australian shearers, rabbit fence and pipeline maintenance patrols, clergymen, and cycle messengers on the remote West Australian goldfields. Fitzpatrick also covers the technological developments, social impact, and sporting and recreational uses, from the first bicycle ascent of Australia's highest peak, to the development of early Australian road maps.

'*The Bicycle and the Bush* represents the discipline of history at its best. Investigative, scholarly, pioneering, but always entertaining.'
—*The Review* (Australia).

'One of the finest books written on sport in Australia.'
—Geoffrey Blainey.

'A highly satisfying piece of original social history.'
—*The Canberra Times*.

CPSIA information can be obtained at www.ICGtesting.com

232058LV00003B/170/P

JUL 1 2 2011

9 780980 748024